brilliant

positive
thinking

Transform your outlook and face the future with
confidence and optimism

Sue Hadfield

Prentice Hall
is an imprint of

PEARSON

Harlow, England • London • New York • Boston • San Francisco • Sydney • Singapore • Hong Kong
Tokyo • Seoul • Taipei • Munich • Paris • Milan

Pearson Education Limited
Edinburgh Gate
Harlow CM20 2JE
Tel: +44 (0)1279 623623
Fax: +44 (0)1279 431059
Website: www.pearson.com/uk

First published in Great Britain in 2012

© Pearson Education Limited 2012

The right of Sue Hadfield to be identified as author of this work has been
asserted by her in accordance with the Copyright, Designs and Patents Act
1988.

Pearson Education is not responsible for the content of third-party internet
sites.

ISBN: 978-0-273-75932-4

British Library Cataloguing-in-Publication Data
A catalogue record for this book is available from the British Library

Library of Congress Cataloging-in-Publication Data
A catalog record for this book is available from the Library of Congress

10 9 8 7 6 5 4
15 14 13

Typeset in 10pt Plantin by 3
Printed and bound in Great Britain by Henry Ling Limited, at the Dorset Press,
Dorchester, DT1 1HD

This book is dedicated to Joseph Finlay Barr – who waited until it was finished before he was born.

Contents

About the author

Sue Hadfield has taught English in comprehensive schools for more than 20 years as well as courses on assertiveness for students and staff. She has also spent the last 10 years teaching assertiveness, creative writing, study skills, and career and personal development at the University of Sussex and to community groups. In addition, Sue delivers workshops helping parents to understand how to help their children to get the most out of school. She believes that being positive and assertive is an essential part of leading a happy, successful and fulfilling life.

Together with Gill Hasson, she has written *Bounce: Use the Power of Resilience to Live the Life You Want* (Pearson Education, 2009) and *How to be Assertive in Any Situation* (Pearson Education, 2010). For more information on their workshops please visit: www.makingsenseof.com.

Author acknowledgements

I would like to thank my family, friends, students and work colleagues for their interest and enthusiasm – and for allowing me to use their stories as case studies. Special thanks to Tom, Christen, Lucy, Karl and Allison Perkin for their perceptive comments, and to Christine Moody and Anne Brown for their kindness and encouragement – particularly after the burglary. As always, thanks to Greg for everything. I couldn't have done it without him.

Many thanks to Sam Jackson for giving me the opportunity to write this book, and to Elie Williams for her help and advice.

Introduction

And I urge you to please notice when you are happy, and exclaim or murmur or think at some point, 'If this isn't nice, I don't know what is'.

Kurt Vonnegut, *A Man without a Country*

Where are you right now as you read these words? You may be in a bookshop or a library – skim-reading before you decide whether to buy or borrow; you may be balancing the book while on the bus or train trying to shut out the noise of the commuters all around you; you may be at home curled up on the sofa or propped up in bed before you go to sleep; you may even be lying on a beach or on a sunbed next to the pool.

Wherever you are right now, you are a fortunate person: you have had an education that enables you to read these words; the curiosity that has encouraged you to examine your attitude to life; a mindset that means you believe it is possible to change; and the intelligence to decide to make that change.

If you are reading this book in any of the situations described, then you probably also have sufficient money to buy a book, to travel, to have a roof over your head and somewhere comfortable to read. Compared with more than half the population of the world, you are indeed fortunate.

This is positive thinking: it is the ability to focus on what you have rather than what you don't have. It is about being aware of when you are happy and being able to appreciate what you have now. It is being able to reflect on things that have happened to you and being able to find something good in even the most painful events. It is about being a useful member of society who cares about other people. It is about looking forward to the future with confidence, because you know that it holds good things for you.

It is human nature to want more than we already have. We believe that more money, a new job, a different relationship will bring increased happiness. The trouble is that once we reach a certain level of comfort, having more doesn't make us any happier. Our standard of living has risen every year for the last 50 years and yet our levels of personal happiness have remained the same. Even people who win enormous amounts of money – or, alternatively, have some personal disaster – report their level of personal happiness is unchanged one year later. This suggests that perceived levels of happiness are not affected by material or physical well-being.

If you think about people that you know, you can see that this is true: their happiness is not dependent on how much they have in a material sense. The difference is that a positive person sees life as an adventure and a challenge and continues to view life in an optimistic way, regardless of either misfortune or good luck. A negative person, however, is inward-looking and sees life in a pessimistic way. Life happens *to* them and seems to conspire to make them more miserable.

The benefits of positive thinking have been the subject of many research studies in recent years. Some of the results need further validation and rigorous examination, but the health benefits of positive thinking are widely accepted. These include: better general health, lower blood pressure, less pain, fewer colds, and more resilience when things do go wrong. People with a positive attitude tend to look after themselves better and so sleep well and generally don't worry so much about the future.

Let's imagine that you can choose what kind of person you would like to be: a positive person, who despite the ups and downs of life manages to look on the bright side and remain cheerful, or a negative person, for whom nothing is ever quite right and life is simply something to moan about. Which would you choose? Which kind of person would you prefer as a friend or partner?

Given the choice, it is difficult to see why anyone would not choose to be a positive person. If you describe yourself as an optimist or a pessimist (or one whose glass is half full or half empty) have you always done so? Perhaps you used to be more optimistic and positive about life, but you have found yourself becoming more negative with each year? The good news is that it is possible to change. However life has treated you in the past, you can change your outlook and become the kind of person you would like to be: someone with a positive attitude who enjoys life to the full. And that's just what this book will help you to achieve.

Of course, this kind of change is not going to happen overnight: like anything really worthwhile, becoming a positive thinker takes time and effort. It means examining your own deeply-held beliefs and prejudices and being prepared to try new things that may be outside of your comfort zone.

This book is going to take you on a journey to becoming a more positive person. And in Chapter 1, I'm asking you to dive right in and visit your past to discover the good, the bad, the painful and the delightful moments from your childhood and how they have shaped your thinking. Your inclination will probably be to miss out the exercises. But remember that you need to confront your usual responses in order to question their validity and bring about change.

In Chapter 2, we will examine the language that you use routinely and the effect that certain phrases and sayings can have on your personality and behaviour. You will find a list of positive aphorisms and proverbs to replace those negative ones that have been undermining your self-belief.

Chapter 3 looks at the research that shows that it is possible to change – even if you have developed the habit of negativity over a number of years. We will consider the effect of aging and whether it is inevitable that we become more negative as we get older.

There is little point in trying to change the way that you think if you don't, at the same time, look after yourself physically. In Chapter 4, you are encouraged to examine your lifestyle and make the changes that will lead to a healthy and happy life.

In Chapter 5, we focus on your dreams and ambitions. Positive thinkers look to the future and make plans to ensure that their dreams are realistic and achievable. You will be guided step by step through the stages that will help you to make your goals in life come true.

Chapter 6 reveals the techniques you need to help you overcome the stress and anxiety that so often seem to dominate life and contribute to a feeling of negativity.

Chapter 7 shows you how to recognise the causes of anger and how to channel it in a positive way so that you can control how you want to respond to the everyday irritations of life. It also includes a quiz, which will enable you to differentiate between the worthwhile and the trivial.

Finally, in Chapter 8, we look at some of the ways that people are tricked into thinking that their lives can change for the better without any effort. We examine superstition and magic, cosmic ordering and fortune-telling and the disastrous effect such beliefs can have on people's lives.

Throughout the book, you will find case studies to demonstrate the benefits of thinking positively, true stories of people who have overcome adversity and gained a positive view of life, as well as inspirational quotations from literature, different religions, and world leaders. And if you want to take your learning even further, I've included some recommendations for additional reading and website addresses, at the end of the book.

So now grab a pad and pen, or get your laptop fired up and sitting beside you. Add to this your own determination to be guided by this book towards leading the fulfilled and positive life that you deserve and let's get going.

CHAPTER 1

Choosing to think positively

Turn your face to the sun and the shadows fall behind you.

Maori proverb

What does it mean to think positively?

Positive thinking is not just the feeling you have when good things are happening in your life – when it is easy to feel optimistic. It is about being able to maintain that feeling of hopefulness and motivation, whatever is happening. It is different from feeling happy – which can change according to events. Thinking positively is a way of being: a way of leading your life.

The joy of positive thinking is that it seeps into every corner of your life. Thinking positively will keep you upbeat about life; it affects your attitude to everything that has happened in the past; and it means you have a healthy, confident attitude about the present as well as being optimistic about the future. It puts you in the driving seat of your life.

---

brilliant questions and answers

Q What about when things go wrong?

A Life holds just as many disappointments, accidents, traumas and loss for positive people as it does for everyone else; the difference is the reaction to these experiences.

It doesn't mean when something dreadful happens you have to think, 'Oh well, better luck next time,' and get on with your life. It does mean being able to deal with misfortune and tragedy, giving yourself time to grieve ▶

and recover, but knowing that you will recover and that life will get better.

Q Is it a selfish attitude?

A Positive people don't go around with a grin on their faces, ignoring the misfortune of others and basking in their own good luck. Being positive does mean valuing yourself, but it also means dealing with other people in a respectful and understanding way. In fact, positive people are more likely to be able to empathise with others and to inspire them. If you have a cynical and pessimistic view of the world, you are unlikely to want to listen to the problems of other people or to have the energy or the inclination to help.

Positive people contribute to the good of society because their attitude to life is one that understands the pleasure of giving rather than receiving. If you have a positive attitude towards your own life and believe that your thoughts and actions can affect your ability to lead a happy and fulfilled life, then you will also want to improve the lives of others and be an active member of society. Contributing to the good of others and to society is one of the defining characteristics of a positive person.

Q Why are some people more positive than others?

A The received, but unproved, wisdom is that we are born with a certain genetic make-up that means we have a tendency to have a sunnier disposition or a gloomier one. It is, however, generally agreed that nurture – your early experiences in life – can outweigh any possible genetic predisposition.

Most children, apart from those who have been abused, neglected or damaged by divorce or bereavement, tend to have a positive outlook on life. If there is anything planned, such as a visit or a holiday, they will expect to have a good time. When something goes wrong, they tend to accept it and quickly resume their previous optimistic view of life. Most children don't expect things to go wrong; they have to learn to be anxious about things.

Q What causes a negative attitude?

A If you were brought up with a family member who always expected the worst and who believed that life is grim, with many obstacles that stand in your way, then it would be very difficult for you to maintain a child's natural happy disposition. If you add to this misfortunes such as illness, accidents or the absent or neglectful parent, then for some people maintaining their equilibrium is an uphill struggle.

No one can do anything about the family and the circumstances that that they were born into. Neither can you do anything about the kind of upbringing that you have had; it's the past and nothing will change what has already happened. You can, however, do something about the way you view your past and therefore about the life you are leading now. As an adult, you can decide that whatever life experience you have had so far, you will use this to make the future better – for yourself and everyone around you.

Q Do you need to deal with the past?

A If you find yourself thinking, 'That's all very well, but I can't get over the anger (or sadness) that I feel about past events', then you need to deal with them first. If you are harbouring resentment towards people who are still in your life, then it will

> if you are harbouring resentment then it will be difficult for you to move forward

be difficult for you to move forward. If you have suffered bereavement or severe trauma, it may be that your feelings are so deeply entrenched that you need counselling or therapy to express your emotions safely.

Unresolved anger can make you bad-tempered and irritable – with the wrong people. You may find yourself being mean or feeling bitter towards people whom you consider to have had a more fortunate start in life. Your animosity may take the form of self-protection: you don't branch out or explore new ideas because you are defensive about your perceived lack of achievement.

If you can't get rid of the skeleton in your closet, you'd best teach it to dance.

George Bernard Shaw, 1856–1950

Being human means living a life that is full of events that shape our characters. No one goes through life without things happening to them, many of which they neither planned for nor expected. If life was predictable, then you would probably be dissatisfied because it was boring. Looking back on your life can be a useful start to change, as it enables you to see the turning points and also to recognise the good as well as the bad.

 **brilliant action**

Part 1: Reflections on your life

It is useful to look back on any family photographs to complete this exercise.

Create a Word document or get a sheet of blank paper and write at the top 'Memories of my life'. Write down three things (or more, if you have a good memory) that you can remember from your early childhood – before you started school, if possible. This could be moving house, an illness, the birth of a sibling, a parent leaving, a holiday, a pet, or perhaps achieving something.

Now write five things for the next ten years of your life. This will include primary and secondary school experiences, but it may also include making and perhaps falling out with friends. Were you ever bullied? Do you remember winning something – or perhaps failing to do so? What positive experiences can you remember? It is usually easier to remember negative ones. What made you feel good about yourself at that age? Put your approximate age next to the memory, if you can.

Now bring your chart up to date with at least another five experiences.

What has happened to you since you left school? There may have been illnesses, accidents and bereavements, but there will also have been births, holidays, achievements and excitement. Highlight the positive experiences in bold, if you are working on a computer; tick them if you are writing by hand. What does the balance look like? If you have many more negative experiences, can you think of any more happy ones to add?

Of the negative experiences, which ones do you think affected you the most? Are there any experiences that you can remember which seemed disastrous at the time, but which you now see in a different light? Which ones do you think are still affecting you now? Is there anything you can do about it?

Some people seem to find it easier to remember painful experiences and have to try hard to remember the sweet ones. Savour and enjoy remembering the happy ones; share them with someone else. Try remembering the good experiences in more detail and see if you can recall the feelings that you had at the time. Fix them in your mind so that you can recollect them whenever you want.

When you have time, examine the photographs and think about the people in them who have helped to shape who you are. Identify three people who have had an impact on you. What positive or negative beliefs do you think they have handed on to you?

Part 2: Become an agony aunt

Sometimes it is useful to look at your life experiences in the third person. Try condensing the highlights (or lowlights) you identified in the first part of this exercise into one or two paragraphs, as if you were writing to an agony aunt. Here's an example:

> Josh was five years old when his brother was born. His mother was depressed for some time after the birth and his father was often absent. When he started school, his teachers found his behaviour demanding as he was always seeking attention and being disruptive. His father alternated between being a heavy-handed disciplinarian when he was around – and not keeping in touch at all when he was away.

▶

Eventually Josh's parents split up. His mother seemed to spend all her time caring for his younger brother and Josh often had to fend for himself. He admits now that he wasted a lot of his time at school and blames his parents for his poor exam results. He has never had a close relationship with his brother and can see that he was jealous of the attention that his brother received.

Josh tends to be quite negative about life and his childhood experiences could be the reason that he finds it difficult to be optimistic and to feel confident about his own abilities as a young adult. His experiences are common triggers for negative thinking. For example:

- A sense of rejection from a parent (which often leads to an unhealthy desire for the approval of others).
- Jealousy of a sibling who appears to get all the good things in life, while you are left to 'fend for yourself'.
- Inconsistent parenting.
- Misbehaving at school in an effort to gain attention (and the inevitable effect of underachieving academically).

Now imagine you are the agony aunt receiving this letter. What would you say to Josh? What questions might you ask him? How can you help him to move forward from the past which is holding him back? Do the same for your own memories and see if you can get a clearer view of your thinking patterns by looking at yourself from the outside.

What can you do?

If you think that you have a negative outlook on life because you still have unresolved problems with certain people or events in the past, then you need to be able to deal with them before you can move on. If you cling on to your hurts – carrying around that 'chip' on your shoulder – you are actually allowing those people or events to continue to hurt you. It means that bully at school is still bullying you 20 years later; your brother's birth is still causing you a problem; your parents' neglect continues to make you feel a failure.

Free yourself

Being able to forgive is the first step in being free of the negative influences from your past. It can be a painful experience to dredge up memories that you would rather

> being able to forgive is the first step in being free

forget. But the fact that you have written them down suggests that you haven't forgotten them. It can also be cathartic to revisit the past – if you give yourself time and understand that you have the power and the maturity to see things differently now.

brilliant tips

Try some of the tips below if you find it difficult to forgive or to deal with painful experiences. They apply to current events in your life as much as the ones in the past. But notice the ones that you reject as being too much effort. No one said it was going to be easy.

1   **First of all, forgive yourself.** Sometimes people who feel negative about themselves have impossibly high standards. No one is perfect and everyone says mean things sometimes; everyone has done things they regret. You are only human: forgive yourself for your past mistakes and unkindness.

2   **Dwell on the positive.** Look back on the list of your life experiences and keep on adding more positive memories, however small, until they outweigh the negative ones. When you find yourself remembering something painful switch to a pleasurable memory. It *is* possible.

3   **Deal with it.** If there is a recurring memory that still has
    the power to upset you or to keep you awake at night, then
    perhaps it is time that you confronted it. If it happened long
    ago you can write a letter – whether you post it or not, you will
    feel better. If it is something recent, then you have to be brave
    and say what you think to the person concerned. Don't be
    aggressive, and make sure you acknowledge how you feel. So
    you could say, 'I felt humiliated when you said that about me.'
    It doesn't mean that the other person will apologise or change
    their behaviour, but you will feel better than if you just suffered
    in silence.

4   **Look for the positive.** Many people have suffered the most
    appalling injustices or traumas and yet have developed
    the resilience to deal with their experiences. A common
    characteristic of resilient people is the ability to look back on
    the event and deliberately find something positive from the
    experience.

5   **Acceptance.** Sometimes you have no other choice but to accept
    that something dreadful has happened. Blaming others and
    bearing a grudge isn't going to change a thing. You are wasting
    your energy being judgemental or negative about something
    you can do nothing about.

6   **Help others.** By turning yourself to the outside world and trying
    to do something good and useful, you will feel better about
    yourself. The best way to stop dwelling on your own misfortune
    is to help others. They don't have to be strangers; your friends
    and family need you, too.

7   **Ask for help.** Confident, positive people are able to recognise
    when they need help and are not afraid to ask for it. When you
    are in a negative frame of mind, you think that asking for help
    is a sign of weakness. Remember: people like being asked for
    help and advice; it makes them feel good.

8 **Forgive others.** To do this you need to try to understand why people behave the way they do. Often, when you put yourself in their shoes, you can see why they behaved so badly. Josh realised as an adult that his mother had suffered from postnatal depression – and had felt bitter that she had to cope with the difficulties of bringing up two boys with no steady income and an unreliable partner.

Examine your beliefs

Fundamental to the way you think are the beliefs that you hold. They hold an enormous power over your life and how you respond to the things life sends you (good and bad).

Every single experience you have had in your life serves to form your beliefs and these beliefs will in turn affect your thinking, in a positive or negative way. So if, for example, you believe that intelligence is inherited (and you think you haven't done very well in the genes lottery) then you won't achieve your full potential. If, on the other hand, you believe that your success or failure is down to you and you want to succeed, then you are more likely to do so.

Your beliefs turn your life into a self-fulfilling prophesy. And beliefs are the most difficult to question and analyse because they have formed and taken root in your subconscious over a long time. Each time something has happened to reinforce those beliefs they have become stronger.

But once you recognise how much they affect your life you will realise how important it is to examine them to see if they are impacting your life for better or worse.

Your negative beliefs tend to be absolute and may feel to you as if they are undeniably true. But they aren't, and, once you have identified them, it is possible to change them. And that will change your whole outlook on life. In the next chapter, we will examine some of the negative beliefs that you may hold and how you can change them.

Recognise your feelings

The first step in this process is to become aware of your feelings and your emotions when faced with a potentially difficult problem or opportunity. By recognising your emotional signals, you will be prepared for your response to a situation.

This doesn't mean never feeling angry or sad. Sometimes, we deliberately listen to sorrowful music because we want to feel sentimental or nostalgic; we leave the cinema after crying, saying how much we enjoyed the film – just as we watch comedies or comedians because we are in the mood for laughing. In these situations, we know what we are doing: we have chosen to play the sad music or to go and see the harrowing or exciting film because we want to feel these emotions.

We all smile, laugh and cry involuntarily because of things that are said or done to us in the present. But we can also react in the same way to a memory. You can conjure up physical feelings just by thinking about something that has happened in the past: an embarrassing situation can make you want to squirm and your heart race even when recollected years later. Negative emotions such as anger, fear and disgust aren't necessarily to be avoided; they can be useful, because they act as warnings against danger or aggressors and alert us to be cautious.

But thinking about the future sometimes causes feelings such as anxiety; negative thoughts about things that haven't happened and might never happen. Common physical sensations that are the telltale signs that you are confronting or thinking about difficult situations are: sweating, blushing, shaking knees, migraines, butterflies in your stomach, feeling sick, a tingle down your spine, or even a rapid heartbeat. All these sensations alert you to the fact that you are feeling uncomfortable, afraid or, perhaps, excited.

These feelings can be useful signs of danger: instinctive reactions that are warnings that you do not feel safe – for example, if someone you have just met offers to give you a lift home. If we didn't have anxiety, then we wouldn't lock our doors or buy insurance. But being able to use our feelings to enable us to take precautions and use common sense is different to giving in to anxiety when there is no physical danger – just a fear that you may make a fool of yourself or perhaps fail at something.

So, for example, if your previous reaction when you felt yourself getting overheated in an argument, or upset by unfair criticism, was to find yourself going red or developing

> you will recognise the signs immediately and know to calm down

a headache, you will recognise the signs immediately and know to calm down, take a few deep breaths, saying nothing until you are composed. Just remember that these physical reactions are being experienced by you – other people don't usually notice them. And even if they do, so what?

Identify your thoughts

Whenever your body gives you these physical sensations, you will have accompanying thoughts racing through your mind. So if, for example, you speak up at a meeting and feel yourself blushing, you may be thinking, 'Everyone's looking at me. Who do I think I am? It's a stupid thing to say anyway.' Or if you take something back to a shop and want your money back, you might find yourself speaking too quickly or your voice shaking. Your inner voice will be saying, 'I'm not going to get my money back. She'll get the manager and there'll be a scene and everyone in the shop will be looking at me.'

The trick is to practise altering your thoughts so that you speak up at the meeting thinking, 'I have a right to be heard. This is a good idea.' Or when you step into the shop, you smile and think assertively, 'I know my rights and will just stand my ground. It doesn't matter who looks at me. I feel good about myself.' When you can learn to think in this way, it changes your emotions and the way you feel and react.

brilliant example

Anna was dissatisfied with her job and had been delighted to get an interview with another firm. This is the story that she related to me about her interview:

'I set off from home in good time, but the bus was late and by the time I arrived for the interview I was feeling stressed and in a panic. Nevertheless, I got there on time and someone brought me a cup of coffee. But I was so nervous I accidentally knocked it over and some of it spilt onto my skirt. It made me feel self-conscious during the interview.

'There were four other people waiting to be interviewed for the same job – all men. I discovered that one of them already worked there. So I was pretty sure he would get it. Several times in the interview my mind went blank and I could feel myself waffling. My presentation was okay, but no one on the panel made a comment. I'm sure I haven't got the job. In fact, I don't think I'll ever get another job and I'll be stuck with my present one forever.'

Negative thinking traps

Can you recognise some of the negative thinking traps that Anna has fallen into?

First of all, her overall assessment of the day is negative: she is convinced that she hasn't got the job and seems to have decided this before she even had the interview.

This kind of pessimism is sometimes a self-protective mechanism: you fear that disappointment is imminent so you prepare yourself, as if to soften the blow when it comes. This is fine as long as you are aware of what you are doing. Remember that predicting failure often affects behaviour and sometimes stops people applying for jobs in the first place.

Secondly, there is an implication that Anna believes that they would prefer a man and that the person who already worked there would get the job. This may be true – although she has no evidence of this. But Anna's negativity would have affected her performance in the interview. Next, she sees the lack of comment about her presentation as being a criticism and is unable to give herself credit for the fact that it went well.

Finally, Anna is guilty of viewing the whole event as a catastrophe: 'I'll never get another job.' This is typical thinking for people whose outlook on life tends to be negative: one disappointment or failure is magnified out of proportion until it becomes a life-changing disaster.

Seeing the same events in a positive light

As a positive thinker, Anna would first of all have patted herself on the back for getting an interview. She found out that more than 50 people had applied for the job; so she has already succeeded just by being there. She would have been pleased that she had the good sense to set off early so that she managed to arrive on time, despite the bus being late.

A positive Anna would have made a joke of the coffee spilling: no harm was done and it didn't spoil her chances in any way. She may not have spilt the coffee in the first place as she wasn't stressed and in a panic after her journey to the interview.

She could at least have been satisfied with her interview performance, particularly the way she managed to cover up when her mind went blank. She had obviously prepared well for the presentation – which most people find nerve-racking – and the fact that they made no comment shouldn't deter her from knowing that it went well.

Whether she gets the job or not, Anna could see the whole experience as a positive and worthwhile one because it has made her realise that she wants to leave her old job and that she is certainly a contender for the kind of job that she wants.

If you tend to think like Anna then it seems clear that to think positively about life will take hard work and a real determination to change. It means challenging thoughts and habits that have been developing over a lifetime and knowing that change will not happen overnight. It is possible, though, for even the most negative person to become a positive thinker and if you choose to do so you could completely change your outlook for the rest of your life.

 **brilliant** recap

- You may need to spend some time examining your negative beliefs, as they will have an impact on everything you do

- Your beliefs, emotions and thoughts all act upon each other to create either a negative or a positive feeling

- Learn to recognise the physical signs of your emotional state, as this is when you are likely to respond negatively

- The important thing is to be able to adapt your way of thinking so that you get rid of the old negative views and replace them with positive and motivating thoughts

CHAPTER 2

Is your glass half full or half empty?

To everyone is given the key to heaven; the same key opens the gates of hell.

Buddhist proverb

The language we use in everyday life reflects what we believe is possible and what we will do about it. The classic example of this is when someone says, 'Oh well, I'm just a glass half empty sort of person.' This statement tells us that the speaker feels resigned to their fate, life happens to them and it's just the way they are.

If someone said that they were unhappy you would probably feel concerned and ask them why and then listen to them explain the cause and perhaps help them to find a solution. If someone, however, says they are a 'glass half empty kind of person', your reaction will be just to shrug and accept it: that's their view of themselves and they are entitled to be that way.

There is nothing that will convince someone who has described themselves in this way that it is possible to change – unless they want to be convinced.

In the first chapter, we examined some of the reasons that people may become adults with a negative view of the world. Whatever the reason, the general feeling is that once you believe your glass is half empty, then

> once you believe your glass is half empty, you are limiting your life options

that is the way it will stay. If you describe yourself like this, you are limiting your life options – not only by your view of yourself, but also by telling other people this is your view of yourself.

The way that you think and the way you behave is reflected in the language that you use every day. The reverse is also true: the language you use affects your thinking and the way you behave. So, if you use negative words and phrases, they make you feel pessimistic and dispirited; feeling like this affects the choices you make in life.

How many of these phrases do you use?

1 It's just not fair ...

2 I'm hopeless ...

3 I'll never change ...

4 I can't ...

5 I should ...

6 It's not my fault ...

7 If only ...

8 I wish I'd ...

9 There's nothing I can do ...

10 I ought to ...

If you use any of these phrases on a regular basis, you are perpetuating a feeling of hopelessness and lack of control over your life. Phrases such as 'It's just not fair' and 'It's not my fault' show that you have a tendency to shift the blame away from yourself. Realising that life isn't fair – but that it's not fair for everyone – is all part of being realistic. If you read these phrases again and complete the sentence with something you have said recently, you will see that they make you sound like a victim.

brilliant example

I teach a university course for people who are thinking of becoming teachers. A stumbling block for many of them is the requirement of GCSE maths at grade C or above. When they realise this many of the students say, 'That's it then. I'm hopeless at maths. I might as well give up my dream now.'

When challenged, they usually agree that they didn't like maths at school and gave up trying. I point out that they are now adults who manage a bank account, pay bills, book holidays, organise the family finances, the supermarket shop, work out how many rolls of wallpaper to buy, understand railway timetables, and that they arrive on time to class each week. The new mantra becomes: 'I wasn't very good at maths at school, but I have learned lots since. I'm sure I would be able to cope with a maths GCSE.'

Without fail, all the adults I have taught, who have gone on to take maths GCSE, have not only achieved a grade C or above, but have actually enjoyed it. Achieving something that they believed was impossible has increased their self-confidence in other areas of life and at least two have become primary teachers with maths as their main subject.

If only …

If you find yourself using the phrases 'If only …' or 'I wish I'd …' it implies that you have regrets about the past that are now affecting your present. So you might say, 'If only I'd bought a flat when they were cheaper' or 'I wish I'd had a baby years ago.' These are statements that show that you have not dealt satisfactorily with decisions (or not making decisions) years ago. You could examine your statements and see if there is anything you can do about it now. If there is, then do something. If there isn't, then the only option is to learn acceptance; otherwise, you are spoiling your chance of present and future happiness.

Learned helplessness

By clinging onto certain phrases and sayings, you are not giving yourself a chance to break free from the cycle of damaging behaviour. It is what psychologists call 'learned helplessness', meaning that, even when things are going well, to a pessimist they will seem fated to go wrong, and therefore there is always a fear of the future.

 **action**

Phrases like 'I should …' or 'I ought to …' imply that you have already embarked on the wrong course of action (or inaction). Just saying these words will make you feel resentful and will take away your motivation to do anything. Start noticing now whenever you use any of the above phrases and stop yourself – even if it is mid-sentence. Consciously, replace your negative phrases with more positive ones and you will find your whole mood and outlook will change.

Negative phrase	Positive phrase
It's just not fair	That's life
I'm hopeless	I'll give it a try
I'll never change	I've decided to change
I can't	I can
I should/I ought to …	I will
It's not my fault	I take responsibility
If only/I wish I'd …	Next time/In future I will …
There's nothing I can do	I've done my best

There's no point me trying to …	I'll only fail if I stop trying
I'll never be able to learn/do this	I can learn anything if I set my mind to it
I'm just not lucky	I make my own luck
I'm too old to …	Age is just a number; it's not going to stop me
It will take me too long to …	I'm determined to do this however long it takes
It's just not worth the effort	I'll have another go
I don't have time to …	I'll take the time to …
I'm no good at …	I'll learn from my mistakes
Let's wait to see what happens	What can I do to achieve what I want?
I've made wrong choices all my life	I've learned a lot from my experiences
I blame my parents	My parents did their best
I blame my education	I believe in lifelong learning
I've never had the opportunity	I'm learning to seize the opportunity
I didn't have your advantages	I'm enjoying learning new things

If you hear yourself saying something negative then pause and say, 'Actually, I am going to …' and repeat your newly-learned positive phrase. If you realise later how negative you've been and the moment has gone, don't beat yourself up: no one changes overnight and it means that you are now aware of your habit. In all things new and challenging, it is normal to have setbacks and frustrations – just don't allow them to depress you or to make you feel like giving up.

By now, you will have identified some negative words and phrases that you use and have some positive alternatives to try. You may, however, also be unconsciously repeating your

You may be unconsciously repeating your negative beliefs in the form of sayings and proverbs negative beliefs in the form of sayings and proverbs that you repeat without really thinking about what you are saying.

⟋ brilliant impact

Study the sayings and proverbs below and decide whether they are ones that you have ever used. Put a tick in the first column if anyone ever made this comment to you or about you when you were younger. Add a tick in the second column if you have ever repeated a similar saying. Now add a tick in the third column if you believe the comment to be true.

Saying/proverb	a. Heard	b. Repeated	c. Believed
1. It never rains but it pours			
2. Nothing ever seems to go right for me			
3. I've never won anything in my life			
4. Don't count your chickens			
5. You've got to prepare for the worst			
6. Every rose has its thorns			
7. Some people seem to get all the luck			
8. Pride comes before a fall			
9. No one ever tells me anything			
10. It's always the way, isn't it?			
11. Just my luck			
12. Troubles always come in threes			
13. A leopard doesn't change its spots			
14. Beginner's luck			
15. The devil looks after his own			
16. It's just not worth the effort			

Saying/proverb	a. Heard	b. Repeated	c. Believed
17. Expect the worst then you won't be disappointed			
18. Let's not get our hopes up			
19. You can't teach an old dog new tricks			
20. Little things please little minds			
21. Don't run before you can walk			
22. I'm just waiting for something else to go wrong			
23. Ask no questions and you'll hear no lies			
24. An apple never falls far from the tree			
25. Wonders will never cease			
26. That's for me to know and you to find out			
27. Because I said so			
28. Do as I say, not as I do			
29. Children should be seen and not heard			
30. Stop crying or I'll give you something to cry about			

These phrases, repeated often enough, become lodged in your head and turn from sayings into beliefs. And that's when they have the ability to dampen your spirits and limit your actions and ambitions.

Ticks only in the 'a' column

If you only have ticks in the 'a' column, it means that you have heard these sayings, but they have had no effect on you. Perhaps you were raised in a family that did not use such aphorisms. Or perhaps they used only positive ones. You've had a lucky escape!

Ticks in 'a' and 'b' columns

Study the sayings that you have ticked in column 'b'. If you haven't also ticked that you believe them, it means that you are repeating sayings that you don't actually believe to be true. Look at what they actually mean and, if you don't agree with them, stop using them now.

Ticks in all three columns

If, for example, you have ticked all three columns for number 17 and believe that you should always 'expect the worst then you won't be disappointed', you will be spending a significant proportion of your daily life in a state of dread or anxiety. If you expect the best and it doesn't happen, then you will be disappointed. But you would have been disappointed anyway; just expecting something bad to happen doesn't alter the fact that it happens … and is bad. The worst happens and you deal with it. But at least you haven't spent days or weeks feeling miserable and in a state of trepidation. It's always annoying if you are feeling miserable and someone says: 'Cheer up, it may never happen.' But it is good advice.

Superstitions

Many of the sayings are similar and are simply superstitions. For example, if you have three ticks for number 12 and believe that 'troubles always come in threes', then after two things have happened anything that breaks or disappoints, however small, will confirm your belief – because you have been waiting and actively looking for something to happen. Things break and go wrong in our lives haphazardly (or sometimes because we are tired and stressed) but people rarely say, 'I've had two good things happen; I'm just waiting for a third.' If they did, as soon as something pleasant happened, it would immediately be seen to justify the saying. Why not give it a try?

Some of the sayings are inflicting your cynicism and pessimism on other people. When you say to someone who is full of excitement or enthusiasm, 'Don't count your chickens before they are hatched,' you are immediately taking away their joy and zest for life. Similarly, if someone has just told you of their success at work or in sport and you say, 'Don't forget, pride comes before a fall,' you are allowing your own negativity to take away some-one's pleasure in their achievements.

If you've ever found yourself saying, 'The devil looks after his own' (or a similar saying), what you are actually saying is that you believe that some people are immoral or crooks and that they get away with it. Even if there are some examples of this happening, by saying it you are generalising and forming a jaundiced view of humanity. Similarly, 'An apple never falls far from the tree' asserts that if someone's family has a bad reputa-tion, then none of the members of that family are to be trusted. Such comments are the foundation of prejudice and lead to a judgement based on probably nothing more than one or two experiences.

brilliant disaster

Rob and Aisha were celebrating Rob's recent promotion at work. They were having dinner in a restaurant with some friends, Wendy and Nick, whom they had not seen for some time. Rob was aware that Nick was annoyed by his success. Nick's immediate response was to say, 'Wonders will never cease. I thought you'd be stuck in that job forever.' He went on to give his advice, 'What you should do now is capitalise on this. Make sure that everyone knows who you are and that you go to every social occasion. Don't bury yourself away working; be more aggressive. I've always thought you should get out more.'

Aisha tried to change the subject as she could sense a tension in the atmosphere. She told the other couple that she and Rob were both training for the London Marathon and that Rob was following a strict regime with a chart stuck to their fridge where he awarded himself a tick for every day that he completed his training. Nick's response was, 'Little things please little minds.' When Aisha told him that Rob had already completed one half-marathon in less than 90 minutes, Nick simply said, 'Beginner's luck.'

Later, when they were back home, Wendy asked Nick why he made such mean remarks. He was surprised and couldn't even remember saying them, 'But they're just sayings. They don't mean anything.' Meanwhile, back in their flat Aisha told Rob that she didn't know why they bothered staying friends with Nick as his hostility made her feel defensive and had ruined the evening.

If you think that Nick is just a lone cliché-ridden loser, start listening for comments like these in the conversations around you. Some people seem to rely on such phrases and they become automatic responses to a feeling of envy. By making destructive statements about other people, Nick is not only spoiling Rob's moment of glory, but also ruining their friendship. His comments serve only to make him look small and it is he who will be filled with self-loathing and probably a sense of failure.

On her visit to England in May 2011, Michelle Obama, when asked by schoolgirls at Elizabeth Garrett Anderson School about her relationship with Barack Obama, said: 'The lesson is: reach for partners that make you feel better. Do not bring people into your life who weigh you down.'

So be aware of people who make you feel bad about yourself: those who seem to deliberately upset you and demean you. Avoid those who spread negativity – they are not the kind of friends that you deserve.

 I've learned that people will forget what you said, people will forget what you did, but people will never forget how you made them feel.

Maya Angelou

Negative talk makes you feel unhappy and it's contagious. It is very difficult to raise the mood once someone has begun on a downward spiral of bitter and cynical remarks. It is particularly selfish to make such comments when other people have things to celebrate, as it means that you are imposing your mood on them.

The negative comments that other people make (or that you make to other people) are easier to spot than the ones you make about yourself. Ask the people you trust to help you to spot them and to help you get out of the habit by pointing out every time you make such remarks.

The constant repetition of sayings means that they become entrenched, without you ever really considering whether they are true and whether you actually believe them. Negative words can also have a serious, harmful effect on people and that includes the words that you use when talking to yourself. Sticks and stones do break your bones but remember that words can most certainly hurt you. Many people can't look in the mirror without telling themselves that they are fat or ugly or old (or all three). The irony is that these self-loathing words often drive people to comfort eat (and thereby gain weight) or to look miserable (and therefore less attractive) or even to become ill – as negative thoughts can cause the release of stress hormones such as cortisol (which can lead to high blood pressure).

> negative words can also have a serious, harmful effect on people

brilliant action

When teaching assertiveness to adults, I ask them to work in small groups of three or four and then each person, in turn, tells the rest of their group three things that they like about themselves physically. This causes great consternation and the typical response is, 'Oh no – can't I say things I don't like about myself instead?'

When everyone has taken their turn and finally struggled to choose things they like about themselves, I ask the rest of the group to tell them what they like about that person. The only direction is to be honest and specific. The responses are immediate and sincere: 'I like your shiny hair', 'You have a fantastic figure', 'You've got nice hands, with long, delicate fingers.' The person receiving the compliments is often amazed, even though they know these things to be true. They have spent so long focusing on their perceived shortcomings that they have failed to realise that these aren't what other people see.

The last part of the exercise is for each person to repeat the compliments they have been given in an assertive and convincing manner: 'I'm proud of my shiny hair', 'I enjoy the fact that I'm slim', and so on. The effect is dramatic and many of my students have told me that practising this exercise actually changed the way they felt about themselves and affected their whole outlook.

Everyone is aware of their physical 'faults' and parts of their body and face that they don't like. The problem is that we tend to focus on these and the bits we don't like are what we see when we look at ourselves in the mirror. Try identifying the parts of you that you actually do like and say so out loud. Whenever you find yourself berating yourself for your 'thunder thighs' or 'hair like straw', replace these with your positive comments or supportive statements like, 'I have a clear complexion' or 'My body is strong and healthy'.

Being self-deprecating

There is a certain cultural bias in being able to present yourself in a positive way. In many cultures, it is simply not acceptable to be able to state your talents or good points because it is seen as showing off. In the Far East, it will be perceived as over-confidence and implying that you are untrustworthy. In Britain, we don't like people who boast or those who parade their virtues and assets. But there is a difference between knowing and acknowledging your strengths and being arrogant and conceited.

Vanity and pride are different things, though the words are often used synonymously. A person may be proud without being vain. Pride relates more to our opinion of ourselves; vanity to what we would have others think of us.

Jane Austen

Pride

It is fine to be modest and self-deprecating, as long as you realise what you are doing. We are in the habit of saying, 'Oh, it was nothing', about things we have spent a lot of time on, or, 'Well, I tried my best', when given praise. If your sense of self-esteem is high and you are generally a positive person, then you can afford to be diffident and self-effacing. But for many people negative self-talk has become the reality and phrases like, 'Oh no, it's not; it's rubbish' or 'I know I won't be able to do that' or 'I'm stupid' are their stock phrases and define who they are both in their eyes and in the minds of other people.

Notice if you are in the habit of deflecting compliments with phrases like, 'This old thing?' or, 'Do you really think so?' It is generous to give compliments and denying or contradicting what the other person has said to you can be hurtful to them and will certainly make them think twice about complimenting you again. If you recognise this behaviour in yourself, then it is possible to change. Decide from now on that every time you receive a compliment you will respond with a smile and a simple, 'Thank you'. Most of all, decide you will savour and enjoy the compliment.

 **definition**

Self-fulfilling prophecy

The term 'self-fulfilling prophecy' was coined by a sociologist, Robert Merton, in his book *Social Theory and Social Structure* (1949). He defined it as being a false prophecy or prediction that is made true by the person's actions. In other words, just by hearing something stated, whether true or not, affects someone's conscious or unconscious actions so that the statement becomes true.

There have been many experiments since to test the theory. Two Americans, Robert Rosenthal and Lenore Jackson, conducted the most famous one in 1968. They gave some primary school children a test and told the teachers that the results of the test showed that some of the children were unusually clever (in fact, they had average scores). They gave these names to their teachers and when they returned to the school a year later they tested all the children again and found that the ones they had singled out to their teachers had improved their scores far more than the other children.

Sometimes you find yourself stuck with a label or description from childhood. So, for example, you might have been 'the lazy one' or 'the sporty one', or perhaps 'the cheeky one'. And these words can become self-fulfilling: you have heard them so often you believe them and the consequence is that they limit your view of yourself. For example, if you were 'the sporty one' in the family, the implication is that you weren't as clever as your siblings and this could have had an effect on the effort that you put into your schoolwork.

If your family still uses outdated descriptions of your behaviour (or appearance) – and you feel they are no longer true – then the next time anyone says it, gently but assertively point out that you have grown up since then and the description no longer applies to you. You could say, 'Yes, I always used to be late but I'm working on it and I'm usually punctual these days.'

In the same way, don't label yourself. You are not the person you used to be if you choose not to be. If you begin a phone call with the words, 'It's only me ...' you are saying that you are not very important in the other person's life.

Be careful, too, that you are not guilty of labelling other people – particularly if you have children. Self-fulfilling prophecies are very powerful and mean that you may need to examine the language that you use about others as well as about yourself.

Positive proverbs

If you have decided that you are no longer going to repeat those negative proverbs and sayings you may want to replace them with more positive ones. It is interesting to note that, despite the different kinds of social communication that we have today, ancient proverbs and sayings are still widely used in all countries of the world. Quotations from famous people whom we admire have also become the shorthand form to confirm what we believe. Think about what the following proverbs actually mean, choose your favourites – and use them. In time you will automatically use these positive maxims and they will have an uplifting effect on your thoughts.

1   Failure is the mother of success. Japanese proverb

2   When the sun rises, it rises for everyone. Cuban proverb

3   Diligence is the mother of good luck.

4   The glory is not in never falling but in rising every time you fall. Chinese proverb

5   Since the house is on fire let us warm ourselves. Italian proverb

6   When one door closes, another one opens.

7   A journey of a thousand miles begins with a single step.

8   Never worry worry – until worry worries you.

9   Laugh and the world laughs with you; cry and you cry alone.

10   A problem shared is a problem halved.

11   An ounce of prevention is worth a pound of cure.

12   Better to light a candle than curse the darkness.

13   Every cloud has a silver lining.

14   Count your blessings.

15   Forgive and forget.

16   Failing to plan is planning to fail.

17   Genius is one per cent inspiration, 99 per cent perspiration.

18   If at first you don't succeed, try, try, try again.

19   Honesty is the best policy.

20   Imitation is the sincerest form of flattery.

21   No one can make you feel inferior without your consent.

22   Practice makes perfect.

23   Practise what you preach.

24   Procrastination is the thief of time.

25   Where there's a will, there's a way.

26   Fortune favours the brave.

27   Success depends on your backbone, not your wishbone.

28   We are born. We eat sweet potatoes. Then we die. Easter Island proverb

29   Every beetle is a gazelle in the eyes of its mother. Moroccan proverb

30   Dig the well before you are thirsty. Chinese proverb

brilliant tip

Use the same technique with these proverbs as you did with the negative and positive phrases: choose the ones that are meaningful to you or the ones that contradict any that you ticked earlier in this chapter. Keep a list of them, preferably in a place that you look at everyday; repeat them when you see them. Start using them when appropriate – even if it is only in your thoughts.

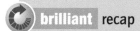

brilliant recap

● Examine the negative language that you use and question any damaging sayings that you repeat out of habit

● Learn to focus on your assets rather than things that you don't like about yourself

● Make sure that you are not stuck with a label that you were given as a child

● Beware the self-fulfilling prophecy

● Replace your negative language with positive words and phrases

CHAPTER 3

Transform your outlook:

Towards a new way of living

Those who wish to sing always find a song.

Swedish proverb

Look back at the sayings and proverbs that you ticked in Chapter 2. Have you ever said, 'You can't teach an old dog new tricks' or 'A leopard never changes its spots'? The implication is that you believe that people can't change. Just having this belief makes it difficult for you to alter the way that you behave.

And, apart from anything else, it's just plain wrong. Brain cells constantly form new connections with each other – giving your brain an infinite capacity to learn and change. So just as you can change your body shape and health by eating better and taking more exercise, you can also improve your mental health by changing your patterns of thoughts from negative to positive.

In his book *A Complaint Free World*, Will Bowen explains that it takes an average of 21 days for new behaviour to become wired into our brains. You can try this yourself by changing your watch onto a different wrist. How long does it take before you stop looking at the bare wrist? Bowen got people to go 21 days without complaining (they were given a wristband that they had to move every time they moaned). He discovered that people were irritable frequently in the first few hours, but less and less so as time went on. After a week, most of them had stopped complaining.

Bowen discovered that stopping moaning and criticising made not only the people taking part in the experiment feel better, but also the others around them. The neuroplastic change in the brain (which has been forced to do things differently) then lays down connections to support the new behaviour. The old pathways don't completely disappear, so sometimes something triggers an old habit – perhaps being offered a cigarette years after you have stopped – and you have to remember the benefits of stopping so that you can choose to say no.

> a habit doesn't change – you just choose not to practise it any more

So when we use the word 'change', it is actually a misnomer; a habit doesn't change – you just choose not to practise it any more. And you may choose to introduce a new one in its place.

For a fascinating account of the curious way the brain works and repairs itself, try *Incognito: the Secret Lives of the Brain*, by David Eagleman.

 Habit is habit, and not to be flung out of the window by any man, but coaxed downstairs a step at a time.

Mark Twain

In fact, trying to implement new habits – such as taking up exercise or eating fruit – can take an average of 66 days before they become habitual, according to research at the University College London led by Dr Phillippa Lally. Her team found that it depended what the new habit was; also, the length of time varied from individual to individual. Happily, they discovered that missing a day made no difference at all. So be prepared for your new regime to take some time to get established and don't beat yourself up if you regress (just get back on the treadmill).

Think of all the new habits that you have adopted since becoming an adult. Most of them will be positive ones that you don't want to change, but they have become habits only because at some time you consciously decided that you were going to adopt them.

For example, when the compulsory wearing of seatbelts in cars was introduced in 1983 (using a series of road safety films featuring Jimmy Savile), most people found it difficult to remember for the first few weeks. Now, when you get into a car, you automatically fasten your seatbelt without even thinking about it.

brilliant example

Many of the products that we use everyday are, in fact, the result of manufacturers encouraging the use of them (such as moisturisers, deodorants, vitamins). Only 100 years ago, few people brushed their teeth. Now we automatically brush each morning and it would be remiss of us to leave the house without doing so.

Manufacturers discovered very early that there was a power in tying certain behaviours to habitual clues through repetitive advertising. When Dr Val Curtis, an anthropologist living in Burkina Faso, wanted to persuade people in the developing world to wash their hands habitually with soap, she approached multinational corporations to ask them for the tricks of the trade in persuading people to adopt new habits. In an interview by Charles Duhigg in the *New York Times* (13 July 2008), she said, 'There are fundamental public health problems, like hand-washing with soap, that remain killers only because we can't figure out how to change people's habits.'

The solution was adverts that showed people walking out of bathrooms with hands that glowed with purple pigment that contaminated everything that was touched. The adverts worked and research showed that the use of soap in hand-washing before meals had increased by 41 per cent.

In the same article, Dr Wendy Wood, a professor of neuroscience and psychology at Duke University, says, 'Habits are formed when the memory associates specific actions with specific places or moods.' She suggests that smokers who try to stop when they are on holiday are more successful because unfamiliar people and places surrounded them. 'If you regularly eat crisps while sitting on the couch, after a while, seeing the couch will automatically prompt you to reach for the Doritos.'

So it seems clear that the best way to get rid of an old habit is to remove yourself from the associations that you have with it. You have to decide whether it's worth missing a few nights out with friends in order to, for example, stop smoking or stick to your diet. If you replace it with a new healthier habit you can see that it would not take long for this to become routine and you will quickly adapt to a new way of living your life.

 **action**

I often hear the comment, 'I wish I'd known that when I was younger' in personal development classes and I encourage the class to compile a joint list of 'Things I Wish I had Known When I was 12' (originally, the age was set at 15, but some said that was too late for them). The list includes things such as, 'Only have sex when you are ready – not to please someone else' (many are single mothers); 'Working hard at school will pay off in the end'; and even, 'Be careful about what you put in your mouth.'

Compile your own list of things you wish you had known when you were younger or that you would like to be able to tell your younger self: it is surprising how revealing this exercise can be about the things in your life that you would like to change. Try watching Sarah Kay's TED talk, 'If I should have a daughter … 10 things I know to be true' (www.ted.com).

 **impact**

Introducing change

In the same way that behaviour becomes a habit and there has to be a deliberate decision to change, these techniques also apply to changing your way of thinking.

Becoming a positive person may mean actually changing your outlook on life and replacing it with a different one. As with most worthwhile things, it's not easy and will take some time before the new habits are established and you can rid yourself of negativity. For any change to be lasting and effective you need to ask yourself these questions:

● What is my motivation?

● Do I believe I can do this?

● Am I prepared to put in the time and effort?

● What help do I need?

● What's my plan?

● Am I prepared to make some mistakes?

● How can I check my progress?

In order to help yourself to change, you have to believe it is possible and you have to be motivated not only to change your way of thinking and behaving, but also to maintain the new habit. It is probable that you are aware of yourself becoming more negative and just believe that life would improve if you could change your outlook.

But if you have any doubts about the motivation for changing the way you think, then it is a good idea to make a list of all the benefits you will enjoy by becoming more positive. These may include:

● Having a rich social life – positive people have more friends

● Being healthier – positive people are more likely to look after their health

● Living longer – negative thinking is a risk factor for many illnesses

▶

- Generating more energy – feeling negative makes you listless and withdrawn

- Mood contagion – your positive mood will affect others

- Helping others – positive people are more likely to be active in their community, because they feel good about themselves

Quite simply, being positive and optimistic will make your life better.

brilliant action: role model

It is also useful to have some role models – people who have managed to change their lives despite disasters and traumas ruining their original dreams and plans.

For example, Liz Murray is a young woman from New York whose childhood was blighted by her drug-addicted parents. From the age of 15, she was living on the streets and in friends' apartments. Her father was living in a homeless shelter and her mother died from Aids. She had barely attended school but someone told her about 'alternative high schools', private schools that accepted people without money if they were sufficiently motivated. She was rejected from several but persevered and was finally accepted at one – where she blossomed despite still having nowhere permanent to live. After a school visit to Harvard University, her teachers encouraged her to apply for one of the six scholarships offered by the *New York Times*. From 3,000 applicants, she was accepted and graduated from Harvard in 2009. In her YouTube video she says, 'I didn't know my chances of success; I only knew that I was going to carve out a life for myself that was in no way limited by the past.'

Start noticing and collecting stories of people who have overcome adversity and have turned their lives around. They can be an inspiration when times are difficult, because they show what is possible if you are resilient and don't give up at the first hurdle.

▶ brilliant example

I often use the exercise 'Reflections on your life' (as described in Chapter 1) with my mature students. There is usually lots of laughter and tears as people relate the highlights and downturns in their lives.

Kerry began by telling the story of the main events in her life to the rest of the class – passing around photographs as she spoke. She told the usual anecdotes from her childhood, then of meeting Tim at university, and both of them dropping out and going off travelling to exotic countries. The photographs were colourful and joyful: two young people enjoying the freedom of being in love and having no ties. Then came the photos of the baby – born abroad, as Kerry was reluctant to give up their lifestyle.

'Tim wanted to come home. Our parents had never met Jamie,' she said. 'Then Tim started to feel ill. No one knew what it was at first and he tried to carry on. Eventually, he was rushed to hospital and was diagnosed with a blood disorder. He died three days later.

'For a long time, I blamed myself. I felt that if we had come home earlier it wouldn't have happened. I had to return home with the baby and go and live with my parents again. I felt that I would never recover. I kept going over and over what had happened and what I should have done. I felt that my life was over and that I'd never feel like that again.

'I've spent the last five years feeling sorry for myself and angry at the way things turned out. I felt so negative about my life I couldn't see how it was possible to feel any different. When Jamie started school, my mother persuaded me to come on this course. I couldn't see the point but, in fact, it's given me a lot of confidence and I feel that I'm ready now for the next stage of my life. I can see now that I was lucky to have such a wonderful man in my life and lucky that we had Jamie before he died. Most people never have a love like that and I'm determined to live the rest of my life in a positive way, as Tim would have wished.'

Kerry was brave to disclose so much of her life to the class. Sometimes, that is the first step in realising things can change. She said afterwards that hearing the stories of the others in the class made her realise she wasn't the only one who had suffered a great loss and that it was possible to accept what had happened and choose not to let it continue to ruin all their lives.

Before the course ended, she had applied and been accepted by the local university to study law. This wasn't the degree that she was going to do originally – she said she was a different person now. It was what she had always wanted to do, but she had never thought that she had the capabilities. Now she felt more positive about life she also felt more confident about her abilities and was determined to fulfil her dream of becoming a lawyer.

Getting old

we need to adjust our attitudes towards getting old and what it means

One of the reasons that people give for not attempting to change their outlook on life is because they say they are too old. Even if they accept that it is possible to change they think: 'It's too late for me to change now. It's not worth it.' Of course it is worth it: every minute of your life is worth it. We can expect to live longer than at any other time in history and we therefore need to adjust our attitudes towards getting old and what it means.

 I suppose that's why people liked my last book: it was about someone having a pleasant old age. It made people feel it was possible. I didn't expect to start a whole new writing life in my 80s, but I did. That is an astonishing thing to happen when one is old, and it is pure pleasure.

Diana Athill, *Guardian*, 15 August 2009

There seems to be little point in being able to extend our lives with advanced medical science if those extra years are dogged with ill-health and a miserable attitude. In their book *You Can be as Young as You Think*, Chris Middleton and Tim Drake claim our bodies can be ten or fifteen years either side of our actual age because of diet and exercise, but our brain age can vary even more – because it is dependent on our attitude to life. They say that a typical young person is enthusiastic, open, excited, creative, and loves life – whereas a typical old person is defensive, grumpy, anxious, risk averse, and closed down. They claim, however, that this is not inevitable: we can choose to have a positive and vibrant attitude in old age just as we can choose to take care of our bodies.

In fact, recent research indicates that as long as we enjoy good health, companionship and have sufficient money, then we are likely to be happier at 70 than at any other time. The English Longitudinal Study of Ageing tracked more than 10,000 people over the age of 50. They discovered that more than half experienced a sense of increased well-being as they got older, perhaps because they were able to spend their time doing the things they wanted to do (and, presumably, were able to stop doing the things they didn't enjoy).

Looking after yourself now and developing the right, positive attitude to life is your best bet for enjoying a full life in old age. Speaking at the Oxford Literary Festival in April 2011 about his book *You're Looking Very Well: The Surprising Nature of Getting Old*, Lewis Wolpert (aged 72) said that babies born today can expect to live, on average, until they are 106. He added that there seems little point being able to extend our lives if we are not enjoying the benefits of those extra years. At the end of his talk, Wolpert told the audience that the secret to living well in old age was down to three things: having a sensible diet; exercising daily, and maintaining a positive attitude to life.

So, becoming more and more negative and pessimistic as you get older may be accepted in our society, but it is not inevitable or helpful. In other societies, where old people are revered, the difference in the attitude and demeanour of the elderly is notice-able. There are, though, many old people in this country who are role models (like Diana Athill, Tony Benn, and Jimmy Savile – all born before 1927) for remaining cheerful and getting the most out of life right until the end. These are people who don't spend their time bemoaning what they have lost, but being glad that they can still contribute and play a part in society. If you know anyone like this, listen and learn from them: they know the secret – that you must live your life to the very end by focusing on what you enjoy doing, doing things for others and maintaining a positive attitude.

Grumpy old men

In 2003, a BBC television programme was broadcast called *Grumpy Old Men*. It constituted of a number of well-known middle-aged men discussing various issues that irritated them. These ranged from other people's too-loud conversations in res-taurants to mobile phones on trains. The more trivial the topic, the more they ranted and raved. It was funny because most of the subjects they moaned about were familiar ones that we moan about too.

The trouble with watching and listening to so much negativity is that eventually it brushes off onto you. You find yourself moaning and complaining about the slightest thing because it is acceptable – and, hey, it was funny on television. It doesn't take long to absorb this kind of language and to repeat it. Very soon it's not funny anymore; it's just depressing. And it's difficult to escape.

Never forget that the people on television are getting paid for their performance; they are in control and it's a job to

them – not a way of life. Don't get
sucked in to joining in when other
people are moaning; it will leave
you feeling depressed. Change the
subject or walk away: find people
whose company you enjoy and who
make you feel good about yourself.

> find people whose
> company you enjoy
> and who make you feel
> good about yourself

Playing the glad game

In Littleton, New Hampshire there is a festival every summer
called 'The Official Pollyanna Glad Day' in honour of the
author, Eleanor H. Porter, who wrote the book *Pollyanna* in
1913. The book is still in print and tells the story of a young girl
with a sunny personality, whose philosophy of life is based on
the 'glad game' – finding some good in every situation. Pollyanna
refused to let other people's pessimism affect her and expected
people to behave decently and kindly towards each other.

Today the term 'Pollyanna-ish' is used in a derogatory way (by
negative people) to mean someone who is naively optimistic or
relentlessly cheerful. In fact, Pollyanna (or Eleanor Porter) was
ahead of her time. Like Pollyanna, positive thinkers automatically say, 'Well, at least …' or 'I'm glad that …' or 'I'm lucky that
…' whenever something dreadful has happened. You can start
consciously playing the 'glad game' and see if you can spot any
redeeming features whenever things seem to be going wrong.

OhLife.com

One way of keeping track of your mindset and ensuring that
you don't revert to your old, negative ways of thinking is to keep
a diary. If your immediate reaction is to shake your head, then
just try this: aim to write only three things that have happened
each day – but, whatever they are, find something positive to
comment on. So if it rains all weekend you could say, 'At least

I could stay in and read my book without feeling guilty.' If you miss the bus, 'But on the next bus I met an old friend I haven't seen for years.'

If you prefer to work on a computer, then you could try registering with OhLife.com – which is an online diary. Once you have registered, a reminder will appear in your inbox at 8 pm with a random previous entry. You can access all your previous entries – which might make interesting reading as you become more practised at positive thinking. It's worth a try for a couple of weeks at least until you establish your new habit.

 brilliant recap

- Believing that it is possible to change is essential to changing your attitude
- Make sure that you are motivated and prepared for the time and effort it takes
- Look out for role models of people who have shown it is possible
- Ask other people to help you to keep on the right track by reminding you if you revert to your old ways
- You don't have to become grumpy as you get older
- Practise finding something good in every situation
- Try keeping a diary with at least three positive comments each day

CHAPTER 4

Look after yourself:

Feel good about yourself

Fear less, hope more; eat less, chew more; whine less, breathe more; talk less, say more; love more, and all good things will be yours.

Swedish proverb

I'd like to lose some weight and to get fit. I know what I should be doing and yet I continue to miss breakfast because I'm so tired on a morning (I don't sleep very well) and I just don't feel like eating. I have a strong coffee to wake myself up and sometimes another when I get into the office.

I'm always making resolutions about eating healthily, but after a few days I find myself eating one of the cakes that someone has brought in to work because it is their birthday and then I think, 'What's the point?'

I joined a gym at the beginning of the year and managed to go almost every day in the first week. Then I had a lot of commitments at work and so I only went twice in the next couple of weeks. Then I got another bad cold and couldn't go and in the end I just gave up.

I stopped smoking a few years ago and I only have one glass of wine on an evening – more on a weekend. I buy organic meat and vegetables and I buy a sandwich or go to an Italian restaurant for pizza or pasta. My partner and I go out for a meal about twice a week: I can never resist the bread basket and I usually have a starter and a dessert.

Chei, aged 32, web designer

The trouble is that there is little point learning how to alter your thinking so that you become a positive person, if you don't also give the same kind of attention to your body. In Chapter 1, we looked at how your thoughts affect the way that you feel physically – so that, when you are nervous, you might feel sick or, when you are worried, you may get a headache.

The reverse is also true: when you eat too much of the wrong food, it affects your thinking and it is difficult to concentrate. If you have a bad night's sleep, you may be irritable and snappy with everyone you meet. If you don't get sufficient fresh air and exercise, it is difficult to feel energised and motivated. In other words, it is a chicken-and-egg situation: it is almost impossible to have a positive outlook on life if you are not at the same time looking after yourself physically.

Most people, like Chei, know what they have to do to stay healthy. We know about the 'five a day' and that sugars and fat should be kept to a minimum. We know that cigarettes cause chest complaints and lung cancer and that drinking too much alcohol detrimentally affects our behaviour and our livers. We know that eating too much of the wrong kinds of food and taking too little exercise causes us to feel lethargic and to put on weight. We know that being indoors all day, perhaps in a centrally-heated office, and then relaxing every evening at home in front of the television means that we often find it difficult to sleep. We are bombarded everyday with messages about what we should and shouldn't do to keep our bodies healthy and effective. We know it makes sense and yet, somehow, we never manage to maintain our good intentions.

Regular nutrition, fresh air, some cuddles and plenty of sleep are the basic necessities to keep babies happy – and really, as adults, we are not much different. Not only do we fail to give our bodies these simple necessities, but we also abuse them by inhaling noxious fumes, drinking diluted poisons and eating food that is unnecessary for sustenance, clogs our arteries, rots our teeth, and makes us fat.

 You are never too old to set another goal or to dream a new dream.

C.S. Lewis

What can you do?

Of course, it is possible to lead a healthy and happy lifestyle. Lots of people do it. The human body has a remarkable facility for regeneration and whatever damage you have already done to your own body – through neglect, ignorance or abuse – there are always ways to improve. It's never too late to limit any harm you have already done to your body by making changes; you can also reverse the effects of an unhealthy lifestyle. You can become clear-skinned, full of energy and strong within a few months – if you start now. It might not be easy – worthwhile things usually take time – but it is possible. What have you got to lose?

> it's never too late to limit any harm you have already done to your body by making changes

⟨X⟩ brilliant dos and don'ts

Do

If you feel that you could improve the way that you treat your body try following these 10 positive steps for a healthier lifestyle:

✔ **Believe it is possible**

Ironically, one of the main indicators for success in dieting, or leading a healthy lifestyle, is the belief that it is possible. If you think, 'I'll never be able to do this', then you won't. Often, when making New Year's resolutions people say, 'I know I won't stick to them – I make the same ones every year' or 'I don't know why I bother: I know I won't do it, I never do.' Try saying, 'This time I know I can.'

✔ **Be realistic**

One of the reasons that people give up without achieving what they wanted is because they were never realistic aims in the first place. If you are 40, then it is not realistic to want your body to be like it was when you were 16. It is possible, though, to have a well-toned, strong, 40-year-old body.

Sometimes, being realistic just means accepting that you have become older. Stop comparing yourself with a mythical golden age when you were younger, and instead focus on the limitless possibilities of being gorgeous whatever age you are, if you take care of yourself.

It may also mean scaling down your aim: if your previous resolution has been to stop eating chocolate every day – and you've failed every time – then try saying, 'I'm going to enjoy one bar of my favourite chocolate every week.' (Don't try this if you have a serious addiction to drugs – including cigarettes – or alcohol!).

▶

The other thing to remember is to attempt only one improvement at a time. Too many people say that they are going to start exercising, stop smoking, cut back on the alcohol and begin a diet all at once – and then wonder why they fail at them all. Choose one and put all your energies into establishing your new regime before introducing something else.

✔ Make a positive decision

A lot of resolutions and plans for self-improvement are negative in their wording. Research has shown that negative goals such as 'I'll stop eating cake' or 'I don't want to be fat' don't work because all your brain hears is 'eat cake'. So make sure all your goals are positive: 'I'm going to be slim', 'I'm going to try lots of delicious fruit', 'I'm going to get fit' and so on.

Remember: the words you think and speak have a great power over what you do and achieve.

✔ Don't be a perfectionist

You may be a high-achiever who wants everything to be perfect. If you are continually striving for perfection, you are bound to be disappointed – because it's not possible. You can only be the best you can be, but it won't be perfect. Nothing ever is. Be determined to do the best that you can but remember you are only human.

Perfectionists are never happy because they are looking only for the end result. It's good to set yourself goals, but remember that being healthy is an ongoing process – you never achieve it and say, 'That's it. I'm done.' That's why people put the weight back on after a diet. You have to learn strategies to look after yourself and to know what makes you feel good and healthy in the long term.

✔ **Learn from Odysseus**

In Greek mythology, the sirens were seductive maidens who lured sailors to their deaths by their singing. Odysseus wanted to hear them for himself, so he asked his crew to lash him to the mast as they passed by so that he would not be tempted to abandon his ship and join them.

Similarly, you probably know your own weaknesses and the reasons that in the past you haven't succeeded, despite your best intentions. You might know, for example, that when you tried to stop smoking you always started again when you were with certain people or in certain places. The way that you stopped was to avoid those people and places until the addiction had diminished.

Look at the successes that you have had and examine how you achieved them. You can transfer the lessons you have learned to other areas of your life. So, if you are trying to lose weight, or to establish healthy eating, it's probably a good idea to cut out the takeaways and perhaps even eating out for a month or so. To begin a new eating regime might mean not having in the house anything that you want to avoid eating or drinking. Be like Odysseus and simply accommodate what you have learned about yourself by guarding against temptation.

✔ **Have role models**

It's always useful to have role models – whether they are people you know or people in the public eye. Be wary, though, of having actors, models or singers as your role models. Remember it is their business, their livelihood, to look good and to keep in shape. They can afford to spend their time and money on exercising and being fed good food, because if they don't their career collapses.

Notice how often the people who lead a healthy lifestyle are also the people who have a positive attitude towards life. Being

▶

negative affects your belief in yourself and your tendency to be resilient when things aren't going well. In order to persevere with the changes that you are making in your life, a positive attitude is vital.

✔ Delayed gratification

Another reason that people don't maintain their healthy lifestyle is because they are not prepared to put in the time and effort. If you usually just wander round the supermarket putting whatever you fancy into the trolley, then it's a good idea to draw up a list and stick to it, if you want to change your eating habits. Remember that all decisions about what goes into your mouth are made 'at the point of purchase'. In other words, if you buy it, you will eat it. Research some healthy recipes, buy the ingredients, and decide when you are going to make them. It all takes time and effort, but it is worth it.

Most worthwhile things take time and it is much easier to eat a snack when you are hungry than it is to wait and cook a decent meal. Immediate gratification is the reason that most plans fail; people can't wait for the ultimate goal and want to be happy immediately. Freud called it 'the power of now' and compared it with the way that toddlers behave when they want something. (Take a look at the Kids' Marshmallow Experiment on YouTube for an example of delayed gratification.)

Always remember how long it has taken you to become unfit or to put on weight. Allow yourself the same amount of time for improvement. You can see a difference in fitness after only a few weeks of beginning an exercise regime. But remember that the aim is to continue to feel this way.

Don't overdo it or try to rush it. The same is true for healthy eating. The main reason people fail on diets is because they want immediate results. They starve themselves and lose weight, achieve their goal, and go back to their old way of eating. If you see looking after yourself as a lifetime commitment, then this won't happen.

✔ Make a plan

Most people don't make a plan and don't have a contingency plan for when things go wrong. It's as if, despite all evidence to the contrary, people believe that their life ahead will be smooth with no illnesses or upsets to derail them. Part of your plan could be to decide that things will happen, but that you will get back on track as soon as possible. The only way that you fail at anything is by giving up. Chei's problem was that he couldn't keep to his resolution of going to the gym every day. So he stopped going altogether.

If you have decided to introduce regular exercise into your life, then it's a good idea to examine your lifestyle and to decide when you are able to do it. If, for example, you enjoy going shopping on a Saturday, then you'll be too tired for additional exercise. And even if that's when you planned to go to the gym, you will probably end up not going after a few weeks. Try to exercise on your most sedentary days – even if it is just a walk round the block before you go to bed. Don't be too ambitious at first. Just concentrate on establishing the principle that you will, say, do 30 minutes of exercise three or four times a week.

It's a good idea to write down your plan – and put it where you can see it. If you write 'gym' or 'walk' or 'swim' on certain days on your calendar, don't forget to tick them off as you do them.

✔ Ask for help

When you look back on attempts in the past to live a healthier life, were you acting in isolation or did you enlist the help of friends?

▶

Some 'friends' try and tempt you with 'Just one more ...' drink or cigarette or slice of cake. These people are not helpful and you either have to ask them not to, or simply avoid them for a while.

A good friend on the other hand will be keen to support you, but you need to let them know you need their help. This might mean going for early-morning walks with you, sharing a punnet of strawberries rather than a cake, or just being there to give you a kick up the proverbial when your resolve starts to weaken.

Sometimes, strangers are the answer: joining a slimming organisation, a dance class, a walking group, or a sports team might be the motivation that you need to keep you going. If you've never done this before, why not give it a go? It might be what works for you – and, as the saying goes, you'll never know until you try.

✔ Monitor your progress and congratulate yourself

If you don't have a plan or staged goals, then it is difficult to see how you are progressing. With each step of becoming healthier, you begin to take it for granted. If you are focused on an end result, such as weighing a certain amount, then you may never applaud yourself along the way.

If you are aiming for an ideal weight, have some smaller goals along the way and consider how much easier it is to breathe when you run or climb the stairs. Take your measurements at monthly intervals and write them down: notice how you feel when your clothes fit you well or when you go down a size.

If you run or swim, time how long it takes you to complete a certain distance and then again after a month. There is no end result: you are becoming a healthy, fit person and enjoying your progress. Goals are motivating, but you may need to set yourself another once you have achieved your ideal weight or run that marathon.

Reward yourself with a treat – it doesn't have to be something to eat or drink – or at least pat yourself on the back at regular intervals.

 action: Putting it into practice

So what advice would you give to Chei? First of all, he doesn't eat breakfast and relies on strong coffee to wake him up. If you don't eat breakfast, it means that your body goes without fuel for probably 12 hours or more (and no, that mid-morning sugary or salty snack you have because you are hungry is not fuel). This makes you lacking in energy, but the answer is not to drink strong coffee. The answer is to eat. It is a good idea to eat protein for breakfast: eggs or cheese on toast with baked beans would be filling and nutritious. Porridge or muesli with fruit and milk will also give you energy and keep you feeling satisfied.

Chei feels obliged to eat the cakes that are brought into his office, but it is fine to say no if you have decided that you want to cut back on sweet things. No one really notices or cares, if you don't make a fuss. To look after yourself and to stick to your plan, you have to be assertive and stop blaming other people. Of course, if Chei did eat breakfast, he wouldn't need to eat a sugary snack mid-morning.

The next thing Chei does is to set himself unrealistic targets. He plans to go to the gym every day, but then gives up when he perceives that he has failed in his plan. Doing some exercise every day is a good idea, but to avoid boredom and setting yourself up for failure, it is best to think of different activities that you can do.

So, for example, Chei could go for a walk in his lunch hour one day; play squash after work one day; go for a run before work another day; go shopping with his partner on Saturday and still fit in a couple of trips to the gym on the days he does nothing. If you plan to do 20 to 30 minutes' ▶

activity every day and only succeed half the time, you'll still be doing sufficient exercise to keep your body working effectively.

Chei berates himself for not achieving his goals, but he doesn't give himself credit for stopping smoking: this is a great achievement and the one that will make the most difference to improving his health. Anyone who has managed to give up cigarettes certainly has the will-power to do anything else they might decide on to improve their health. Chei could say to himself, 'I was motivated and focused when I stopped smoking and I'm pleased with myself. I know that I can do anything if I set my mind to it.'

Chei could decide to make different choices at lunchtime. If he chose salads and protein at lunchtime instead of sandwiches, pizza or pasta, he would have saved calories for his evening meal. No one really needs a starter and a pudding; he could choose one or the other. If he is serious about losing weight, he could try missing out the wine altogether for a month.

Alcohol just provides empty calories (it has almost as many calories as pure fat) and if you continue to drink but cut back on your food, then you will be hungry and will inevitably break your diet. A pint of lager is about 200 calories – similar to a sugar-coated doughnut – so think of drinking all evening as eating one doughnut after another. Similarly, a bottle of wine is like eating the first layer of a box of chocolates (and two bottles is the equivalent of the whole box). You might enjoy it, but wouldn't expect to lose weight. The charity Drinkaware surveyed 2,000 adults and found that although one in three intended to track their calorie intake over the following month only one in ten of those thought about limiting the alcohol they drink.

Chei finds it difficult to feel positive because he keeps repeating the same mistakes without analysing what works and what doesn't work for him (the definition of madness according to Einstein: 'Doing the same thing over and over again but expecting a different result'). He catches 'another' cold, which suggests that he is often run down. We can't help catching colds if we come into contact with people. But by looking after yourself physically and mentally, you will recover more quickly and so won't be vulnerable to every germ going around. Frequent colds and headaches are a sign that you need to take stock of your lifestyle and make some changes.

brilliant tip

- Aim for 20 to 30 minutes of exercise a day – but make it different most days
- Do things you enjoy and count the exercise you already do
- Cook meals from scratch when you are at home – using unprocessed ingredients
- Eat only one or two wheat-based foods daily: a slice of wholemeal bread, cereal, or pasta (and avoid the bread basket in restaurants)
- Replace sugary snacks with fruit (prepare a bowl of segmented orange, grapes, kiwifruit, strawberries in the fridge for evening snacking) or raw vegetables if you prefer them
- If you want to lose weight, cut out alcohol for a month
- Try replacing coffee with decaffeinated coffee or tea

Sleep

Chei also said that he didn't sleep very well. Of course, eating, exercising and sleeping are all connected and if you eat healthily, don't drink

> there are three pillars for health: diet, exercise and sleep

or smoke, and get outdoors most days, you are much more likely to sleep well. There are three pillars for health: diet, exercise and sleep. And you need all three to support your body in a fully-functioning way. Most people at least know about how to improve their diet and usually intend to take exercise, but very few of us know how to get a good night's sleep. Some people seem to be predisposed to insomnia and it is difficult to motivate yourself to follow a healthy lifestyle if you are tired from lack of sleep.

Because of our increasingly sedentary lifestyles, it is usually mental tiredness that people feel rather than physical exhaustion. You go to bed after being on the computer or watching television and your mind is still racing. Or you fall asleep easily and then wake up in the small hours, going over what you should have said at work or anxiously going over the day ahead. There is nothing more frustrating than lying in bed just waiting for sleep to overtake you and being unable to do anything about it as you lie there wide awake.

What are the consequences of poor sleep?

There tends to be an attitude that it is admirable to require little sleep (politicians and workaholics frequently boast of how little sleep they need). However, there has been extensive research to show that not only can lack of sleep shorten your life, it can also affect your capacity to learn, and lead to a more negative outlook on life.

the work–life balance is causing too many of us to trade-in precious sleeping time

Research at Warwick University (based on 475,000 people, in eight countries, tracked between seven and 25 years) indicates that less than six hours of sleep a night can shorten your life. The researchers discovered that people who slept for less than six hours were almost 50 per cent more likely to develop heart disease and 15 per cent more at risk of strokes. Professor Francesco Cappuccio, who conducted the research, observed, 'The work–life balance is causing too many of us to trade-in precious sleeping time to ensure we complete all the jobs we believe are expected of us.'

The Great British Sleep Survey, published in February 2011 by the sleep organisation Sleepio, revealed that – compared with people who sleep well – insomniacs are three times as likely to experience low moods, lack of concentration, and difficulty in getting things done. They were four times as likely to have relationship problems and more than twice as likely to suffer from lack of energy.

brilliant example

In their book *NurtureShock*, Po Bronson and Ashley Merryman discuss the devastating effects of lack of sleep on children's capacity to learn. The effect of not getting enough sleep affects not only their memory, but also what they remember. They discovered that sleep deprivation means that negative memories are recalled more easily than positive ones. The authors cite an experiment by Dr Matthew Walker, of the University of California, where sleep-deprived college students were given a list of words to recall. They could remember 81 per cent of the words with a negative connotation, like 'cancer', but only 31 per cent of words with positive connotations, like 'sunshine'.

In other words, not getting sufficient sleep may be a contributory reason for having a negative attitude towards life.

How much sleep do you need?

The average adult sleeps for about seven hours, but there is a wide variation; to sleep straight through for eight hours is quite unusual. The amount of sleep you need varies according to age and depends upon what you do during the day. Newborn babies sleep about 17 hours out of 24 and a 10-year-old will sleep about 10 to 12 hours. The older you get, the less sleep you need – and the more fragmented and lighter the sleep becomes.

Expecting to sleep for a straight eight hours every night is one of the reasons people get frustrated about their lack of sleep: aiming for the unattainable causes anxiety – which keeps you awake (and seven hours is all you need). The more you think, 'I must get to sleep: I have a big day ahead of me tomorrow', the less likely you are to fall into a deep untroubled sleep.

Sleeping pills

If you look round any health food shop or chemist's shelves, next to the diet aids, you will see rows and rows of different kinds of herbal sleeping remedies. About 4,000 people a year call the insomnia helpline and an increasing number visit their GPs for help in getting a good night's sleep. GPs get only a total of about five hours' training on managing sleep disorders and so there seems to be a tendency to rely on medication. According to a survey conducted by Surrey University, published in February 2011, one in eight people don't get six hours sleep a night and one in 10 people rely on medicine to get to sleep.

Medication gives you a drug-induced sleep rather than a natural one, and sleeping pills are addictive. They can be successful in treating insomnia in the short term, but the tolerance level declines very quickly. After a month, they lose their effectiveness – and within a year they could be doing you more harm than good. By this time, you will probably be dependent on them and stopping them causes withdrawal symptoms. Unfortunately, the main withdrawal symptom of sleeping pills is insomnia. It seems that the only way to establish good sleeping patterns is to examine your lifestyle and make some changes.

How to fall asleep

We'd all like to get into bed and fall into a deep, trouble-free sleep – waking refreshed and energised in the morning.

Similarly, if you do wake up in the middle of the night, it would be a comfort to know that you just have to roll over and you'll fall back to sleep in a few minutes. The problem is that once morning comes, you get up and get on with your day without giving the following night any serious thought. And so the pattern repeats itself night after night, with you becoming increasingly frustrated – but probably not devoting any daylight hours to solving the problem.

Some of the following ideas may help you to achieve restful and peaceful nights.

 **impact**

Getting comfortable

First of all, make sure that you have all the practicalities covered: a comfortable bed and mattress (if you've had your mattress for ten years, you will have slept on it for approximately 30,000 hours); a dark bedroom, if you prefer it (blackout blinds or thick curtains will do the trick or try an eye mask); the right temperature (about 18°C is ideal); and, of course, peace and quiet (ticking clocks and snoring can drive you mad at 2 am – you may need ear-plugs). Clean sheets and pillowcases also seem to make a difference.

Write it down

If you've got all this in place, the next obvious source of wakefulness is anxiety. We will be looking at techniques to deal with this in Chapter 6. Meanwhile, a useful trick is to keep a notepad and pen by your bed and simply write down what you are worrying about. Tell yourself that there's nothing you can do about it now – you know what the problem is, you've recorded it, and you will deal with it in the morning. You can also download a sleep diary from the Mental Health Foundation's sleep website: www.howdidyousleep.org.

▶

Get rid of tension

Sometimes, when you are lying awake, you are not aware of the physical tension in your body. Some people grind their teeth, even when they are asleep; others clench their jaws, hunch their shoulders, or form their hands into a tight grip. The best way to discover if part of your body is tense, and to learn how to get rid of this tension, is deliberately to tense the whole of your body.

This takes a few minutes and it's best to practise during the day – when you are not trying to get to sleep. In fact, it's a useful exercise for any time that you are feeling particularly tense and need to relax. Start with your feet and clench and curl your toes, work your way up your legs, trying to tense the muscles in your calves and thighs and then your buttocks. Then clench your fingers, so that you form a fist, and tense the muscles in your arms and then your shoulders, and then your neck and your jaw. So for a few seconds the whole of your body is tense.

Then begin to relax each part in reverse order. Do it slowly and try to enjoy the feeling as you release the tension. Usually, you will have become aware of the parts of your body that you have been unconsciously holding rigid and it will be a relief to relax, say, your jaw or your shoulders. You can repeat the whole process as many times as you want but be careful not to rush the relaxing – don't let it all go at once.

Yoga

Studies at Duke University, North Carolina and the University of Miami have shown that yoga can be effective in the relief of chronic muscle pain, fatigue, insomnia and hot flushes. The research showed that yoga was useful in reducing the discomfort of lower-back pain, as well as alleviating pain in the joints of those suffering from osteoarthritis.

Although some kinds of yoga can involve strenuous and demanding positions there are other kinds, such as Hatha yoga, which are more gentle. Hatha yoga teaches you to adopt positions that improve flexibility as well as concentrating on breathing exercises, relaxation and meditation. Because this type of yoga involves the motor and sensory nervous systems it helps induce deeply relaxed states and leads to a significant reduction in discomfort and the need for pain killers.

Achieving a quiet mind

If you already practise yoga or meditation, then you will already be using the following techniques and probably don't have any trouble in getting to sleep. If, however, you find yourself lying in the dark with your mind teeming with chaotic thoughts, then you may still find it difficult to get to sleep by physically relaxing your body as described above. Again, this next step may take some time to achieve – but it seems to work for many people.

Once your body is relaxed, picture yourself somewhere safe and warm – preferably a place that you have actually experienced. So let's imagine you are lying on a beach: the sun is warm on your back, you can hear the sea, and there is absolutely nothing for you to worry about. Now concentrate on your breathing. As you breathe in, think 'in' silently to yourself – and as you breathe out, think 'out'. Persevere: other thoughts will try to come crowding in, but if you keep thinking 'in', 'out', in time with your breathing, then it is impossible to think anything else. It takes practice, but it does work if you give it a chance. There are more tips on simple breathing meditation in Chapter 6.

 **brilliant** recap

- Looking after yourself is important to positive thinking
- Most sleep problems are temporary and caused by anxiety – use relaxation techniques or try writing down your thoughts
- Video games, checking emails, texting, even watching television just before you go to bed can interfere with sleep
- Make sure you get some fresh air and exercise every day – but not just before you go to bed

▶

- Eat nutritious food – a strict diet will mean you are hungry – carbohydrates help you to sleep (try a small bowl of porridge or rice pudding)

- Rich food also keeps you awake – have your evening meal at least three hours before you go to bed – and keep it simple

- Try not drinking alcohol at all for a month (it causes dehydration and you wake up because you are thirsty – or need the loo)

- If you are suffering from long-term insomnia then see your doctor – there might be something that you've overlooked

CHAPTER 5

Goals and purpose:

Give your life direction

We know what we are, but not what we may be.

Shakespeare, *Hamlet.*

Having goals and purpose means sorting out what you value most in life and pursuing a life that enables you to live according to those values. It usually means having aims and ambitions that will give you a sense of purpose and enjoyment in life. Having goals and purpose in your life often makes it easier to focus on what you want and keeps you on a positive path. Having a goal doesn't necessarily mean that you decide that you want to be a concert pianist and your whole life becomes directed to that one aim (although it could).

What are your values?

How do we know what we believe and what we want from life? We often find it difficult to articulate what our values are. We live from day to day, often not really thinking or questioning what we are doing until we are faced with a crisis. It is when things go wrong – a relationship breakdown, being made redundant, an accident, or a natural catastrophe – that we suddenly question what our life is really about and begin to examine what we want from life.

Terminal illness or the death of someone close seems to inspire people to think about, often for the first time, what really matters in life. The book *One Month to Live: Thirty Days to a No-Regrets Life* became a surprise best seller for Americans Kerry and Chris Shook when it was published in 2008, when they asked the question: 'If you only have one month to live, what would you change?' Similarly, a popular blog written by Patti Digh (37days. typepad.com) after her stepfather was diagnosed with terminal cancer posed the question: 'What would I be doing today if I only had 37 days to live?'

Addressing these questions doesn't mean living every day 'as if it were your last' but it does mean that instead of letting disasters rule your life, you could look at them differently and treat them as a chance to change course – to re-evaluate and consider a different way of being.

Moral legacy

In her book *Intimate Death: How the Dying Teach Us How to Live*, Marie De Hennezel, a French psychologist, describes how she works with the terminally ill in Paris. She helps them to confront their fears and to live their final days in serenity and peace. Most of them are poor and feel that they have failed their families, as they have very few valuables to leave them. She encourages them to realise that they are bequeathing something more valuable than material possessions: the wisdom of their lives. When asked how they wanted to be remembered, they said, 'As someone who has led a loving, giving and moral life', 'Someone who was happy and fun-loving', and 'Someone who was a good grandparent' or 'A loving wife'.

Most of us would like to be remembered for the way that we lived, rather than because of the things that we have acquired during our lives. Leading an authentic life means knowing what your values are and being true to them.

 **example**

Values

Dr Martin Seligman, an American psychologist, coined the phrase 'learned helplessness', highlighting how some people who are ground down by seemingly insoluble problems become literally helpless: they become more passive, more anxious, slower to learn, and sad. Seligman realised that it was possible to change this kind of outlook. Nurturing our inner strengths and social intelligence helps to make people more resilient and develop a more positive outlook on life.

Seligman raised millions of dollars to fund his research and involved 150 scientists across the world. The research also included studying works ranging from Confucius to Aristotle. The principle behind the thinking was that previously psychologists had studied only what made people unhappy and negative about life; instead, Dr Seligman and his colleagues were studying what made people happy and have a positive outlook.

They recognised the six core virtues that positive people (throughout history and in different cultures) have in common. These virtues were further subdivided into 24 strengths, which can be useful when examining your own set of beliefs and values.

Which of the following virtues do you think are important to you? Which do you think are the ones that others would use to describe you?

- Wisdom and knowledge: this includes having a love of learning; being open-minded; having perspective; valuing curiosity; being creative.
- Humanity: this means having social intelligence; love and kindness.
- Justice: this includes a sense of fairness; the importance of citizenship, social responsibility, leadership, loyalty and teamwork.
- Temperance: this means being able to forgive; having mercy, humility and modesty; self-control and prudence.
- Transcendence: this includes gratitude, hope, humour, spirituality and the appreciation of beauty.

▶

● Courage: this means being brave; having persistence, integrity and vitality.

Dr Seligman's books are well worth a read to gain a deep understanding of authentic happiness. I'd also recommend a visit to his website (www. authentichappiness.sas.upenn.edu) where you can take the 'optimism test', the 'work-life questionnaire' or try the 'compassionate love scale'.

What do you enjoy?

The UK Office for National Statistics has created a 'wellbeing' index as a part of the Government's Integrated Household Survey to gauge the nation's happiness (www.ons.gov.uk/wellbeing). Typical responses when asked 'What makes you happy?' were simple things like the smell of fresh coffee, a walk in the park, and a plunge in a swimming pool. The replies to the question 'What things in life matter most to you?' included having the freedom to do as you choose and having a park at the end of your street. Creating a 'gross domestic happiness scale' for the whole country is an interesting exercise, but it is also useful if it makes you stop and think about what proportion of your life you spend doing things that you value and enjoy.

> how many hours each week do you think you spend doing things that you really enjoy?

How many hours each week do you think you spend doing things that you really enjoy? Think of the people whose company you enjoy the most – how many hours a week do you spend with them? If you feel that you are spending more time doing things you don't want to do – with people you don't want to be with – it may be time to examine your priorities.

Can you remember the dreams and ambitions that you had as a child? Ask most children under the age of 11 and they will have a very clear idea of their future. Ask them what they want to be and they know: they are not inhibited by the job prospects, how long the training will take or what it will cost or whether they will be able to do it. Their dreams and desires may change from year to year, but their conviction that they can become an astronaut, or a lawyer or a pop star is not diminished by any sense of fear or doubt about their abilities and talents.

Give yourself some time to do the next exercise and allow your imagination and your sense of self-belief to become as strong and free as when you were a child.

brilliant exercise

1   Recollect what has previously given you purpose.

    What made you feel fulfilled in the past? What gave you the most pleasure when you were younger?

    Write a list of the things that you used to enjoy:

    What lessons did you enjoy the most at school? Art classes? Singing in a choir? Being in the school play? Playing team sports? Tennis?

    Swimming? Gymnastics? IT? Learning a foreign language? English?

    What about out of school? Listening to music? Dancing? Writing poetry?

    Photography? Growing things? Cooking? Reading? Playing the guitar?

    Which of these do you still do? Which ones could you do? Which ones would you like to do? Why don't you do them?

2   Next, think of the present.

    What do you enjoy doing?

    What can you do? What is satisfying in your life at the moment? What makes you feel good about yourself?

Make a list of the activities that you do now, that you enjoy (and that probably have nothing to do with your paid work).

3   In the future.

What would you like to do?

You need to have time to let yourself think and to let your imagination wander. It is useful to discuss this with other people as their ideas might spark some of your own.

The American psychologist, Professor Abraham Maslow, made a study in the 1950s of successful and fulfilled people. His conclusion was that this was the natural state for all humans and that we could all be effective and fully accomplished in this way. He presented his 'hierarchy of needs' as a triangle, with our basic human needs, food and water, at the bottom. Next came shelter, safety and clothing. And above that the social needs of belonging to a group.

The next tier is our desire for self-esteem. When this need is satisfied, and we no longer need to prove ourselves to others, then we can progress to the top of the triangle – what Professor Maslow called 'self-actualisation'. This is the need for meaning and purpose in life: our work, our activities and our existence are in line with our declared values and ethics. It includes the need to do things for other people: to be altruistic and caring. According to Professor Maslow, this is the highest state that humans can achieve and it is possible for us all to achieve it.

 Life isn't about finding yourself. Life is about creating yourself.

George Bernard Shaw

Dreams, hopes, goals and ambitions

Having first considered your own values and beliefs, it is useful to look at the things that you enjoy doing and to see how these fit together when making goals that are personally significant for you. Remember that working towards goals is one of the main ways to create a feeling of optimism and purpose. Some of your goals will change as time goes by and some you may never achieve, but you certainly have more chance of achieving something and leading a more purposeful and positive life if you have a clearer idea of what you would like to accomplish.

Now make a list of all the things that you have ever dreamed that you would like to do with your life. Some of them may be small and quite quickly achievable, whereas others might be lifelong plans. Imagine looking back in 20 years at what you have done with your life. Where would you like to be? What would you like to have achieved? Which relationships do you hope have endured? What new relationships do you hope to have formed?

If you find that your list includes your hopes and ambitions for your children or partner, then have a separate one for them. Try to think of 10 to 20 things that you would like for yourself.

 **example**

Some ideas

Here are some ideas that other people have shared with me:

own my own place	find a partner
learn to play the piano/guitar	design and make my own clothes
water-ski	help at a homeless shelter
be able to speak fluent Spanish	take good photographs
go away for the weekend with my friends	get a well-paid job

▶

work for VSO	live in Paris
visit Buckingham Palace	go to an opera
lose weight	run a marathon
be involved in my local community	have a close relationship with my family
improve my qualifications	volunteer at the local hospital
learn to cook	become friends with my ex-husband
give dinner parties	write a novel
become a party activist	visit America/Australia/China
learn to sail	pass my driving test
have a few hens	run my own company
improve my fitness	

Let your imagination run free – forget how much it would cost or how long it would take. You don't have to share your dreams with anyone else; there is no one to impress. Forget about failing; forget about what you think you 'should' do with your life and think about what would make you feel good about yourself.

Keep looking back at the values that you listed as being important to you. No one can stop you having dreams and if you don't dream, how can you know what you want?

Keep the list ongoing: add other things as you think of them (put the date at the top of your list and again next to any new ideas). You may have a whole set of different goals in 20 years' time. Many of your wishes will have a clear end goal (such as 'pass my driving test') but some things (such as 'maintain a good relationship with my parents') might not have an end date. It's not like shopping, where you just buy something you want and that's it.

Next, choose a few things from your list and put an estimated deadline next to each item. Be realistic about how long it will take to get to where you want to be. (I still have my list from 20 years ago.) Now, take a cool look at your list and decide which ones are the most realistic at this point in your life. For example, 'live in Paris' might not be possible at the moment, but may be something you could do at another stage of your career.

Ask yourself, 'If I achieve nothing else in the next few months except this …', what would it be? This is going to be your first goal, but you can repeat this technique, over time, with every item on your list. This is your life and you only live once. Make sure you have no regrets.

 **action**

Let's imagine that you have chosen: 'learn to play the piano' from your list:

Goal

Ask yourself: What is my goal? 'Learn to play the piano' is too vague. Do you want to be able to perform to the public, or get to Grade 8 exam level, or play well enough for your family to be able to sing carols as you play at Christmas? Clarifying what you want is important for your sense of achievement.

Strengths and achievements

Now analyse the strengths that you already have that will enable you to achieve your goal. Think of something that you have learned to do, for the first time, as an adult and how tenacious you were. It may be that you had piano lessons when you were younger, or perhaps you can already play another musical instrument. As an adult, you have more control over your time – you won't be told when you should practise. Remember – you are doing this for yourself – and that in itself is a strength.

▶

Challenges

You will probably find it very easy to think of reasons why you can't fulfil this dream. The main challenge for adults is often that they don't have the time. It may be that you don't have a piano – or room for one. The cost of lessons may put you off. Annoying the neighbours when you practise might be another barrier.

Solutions

Finding solutions to problems requires positive thinking. If you believe that it is possible, then you will find a way round the obstacles in your path. For example, you may know someone with a piano who would allow you to use it (think of something that you could do in return). You could think of a way to earn some extra money for the lessons, or to buy a piano (keep the money as a separate fund). You could buy a digital piano – which has earphones – to solve the noise problem. Finding the time usually means cutting out something else. Perhaps you could limit the television or time on the computer.

Next step

Now you need a plan of action. There will be different ways of achieving your goal and you need to find out what the options are. Do some research to find out how much second-hand pianos cost. Don't forget to look on websites such as Freecycle (www.uk.freecycle.org) – on this site there are also adverts offering, for example, to exchange Italian lessons for piano lessons. You could look at the small ads in your local newspaper or newsagents for casual work, such as babysitting or leaflet distribution, for a quick way to earn the money you need.

Now

Once you have made an action plan make the first step immediately – before you have time to procrastinate. This could be looking on useful websites or buying your local paper to see what there is available in your area. If you are aiming to earn extra money, give yourself an amount and a date to aim for.

Make sure that you don't take on too much all at once. Aim to have one major long-term goal that you keep working towards and then perhaps two or three smaller goals over the

> make sure that you don't take on too much all at once.

next three months. Don't forget to check how you are getting on and that you are actively doing something. Set a date – perhaps a month ahead – to see what you have achieved and what you need to do next. Ask yourself, 'What is it most important for me to achieve next?'

Prioritise your chosen activity; the reason you haven't achieved it already is because you have allowed other things to get in the way. It is very easy to slip back into your old ways and just let life pass you by in a passive and hopeless manner. If you find yourself stuck at any stage of your plan, ask yourself, 'Am I going to give up this dream?' It may be that it's not the right time. Only you can decide what you want to do with your life.

Writing down your dreams and goals is usually the last exercise I ask my students to do at the end of any personal development course. This is to ensure that students leave with a sense of purpose and that they have a plan for what they would like to do next. In one class, as everyone was busy writing and concentrating, I noticed that Lorraine, who had four children, had taken herself off to a corner of the room and had her back to everyone. I asked her if she was okay and when she turned round I realised that she had tears streaming down her face.

When Lorraine had composed herself, she showed me her sheet of paper. It was completely blank. Finally, she said, 'I have no idea what I want. I seem to have spent my life trying to please other people and it means I think of myself as a wife and a mother. I can't think of anything that I would like to do just for me.'

▶

Lorraine asked the rest of the class if they would share their goals to give her some ideas. Each person chose three and read them out. Lorraine listened carefully and then finally started writing. The five things she wrote are contained in the list of suggestions I gave earlier. The last one was: 'learn to play the piano'. And I know that she achieved this dream, because three years later she invited me to hear her play in the local community centre.

Visualisation

Another technique that positive thinkers use to achieve their goals is creative visualisation. This means that you imagine as realistically as possible what it would be like to achieve your goal. It is used in sport, for example, by someone taking a shot at the goal, or someone trying to hit a hole-in-one in golf, or perhaps the last stretch of the road when running a marathon.

You can use it to keep yourself going when your motivation begins to falter. Imagine yourself collecting your degree, ordering a meal in fluent Spanish, playing your guitar on stage. Don't just visualise it – use all your senses: hear the noise of the audience clapping, smell the food in the restaurant, feel the strings of the guitar on your fingers.

It may take some practice, but it works for lots of people – so it's worth trying if it helps you to achieve your goals in life.

Living in the moment

Living in the moment means being so engaged with what you are doing in the present nothing else can crowd your mind. Being involved in some of the activities on your list will keep you challenged and absorbed so that it becomes impossible to think in a negative way.

Having goals, dreams and ambitions gives you purpose in life and this, in turn, makes you feel positive about yourself. It is important, though, to realise that it is not the achieving of the goals that makes you feel happy – it is the working towards them. To do this, you have to make sure that you let go of bad memories of past attempts or they will continue to hold you back.

Some of the goals on your list will have been there for some time; you may have been hoping to achieve them for years. If you focus on what has gone wrong in the past, then you will sabotage your dreams for the future. By 'living in the moment', you acknowledge your negative feelings and accept that they are part of the human experience. It is not about having an empty mind, or suppressing your feelings; our minds generate thoughts constantly and as soon as you decide not to think about something, you will think about it. It is about recognising that what has already happened is not going to stop you enjoying life now.

 **brilliant** definition

'Flow'

Mihaly Csikszentmihalyi (pronounced: cheek-sent-me-high-ee), professor of psychology, proposed the term 'flow' for this state of 'living in the moment' or total absorption. The thesis of his book of the same title is that the best way to achieve happiness is by creating the mental state of 'flow'.

Once you are engaged in such an activity, your perception of time changes (it seems to have passed quickly); discomfort goes unnoticed (so you don't realise you have backache or a stiff neck until later); and negative thoughts just don't enter your mind.

Flow is characterised by nine different elements:

1   Clear goals at each step of the way

2 Immediate feedback: knowing that you are doing it properly

3 A balance between challenge and skills: if it is too difficult it
   will lead to anxiety and if too easy it will cause boredom

4 The merging of action and awareness

5 No distractions

6 No fear of failure

7 No feeling of self-consciousness

8 Sense of time is distorted

9 It is done for its own sake (such as playing a musical instrument)

You can go through your own list and see which ones match the criteria for being 'flow' activities. Csikszentmihalyi defines happiness as having an active sense of accomplishment and improvement, whereas pleasure is the satisfaction of basic biological desires or static contentment. So the state of happiness would be at the top of Maslow's triangle, and the best way to achieve it would be through 'flow' (whereas pleasure would be included within physical needs).

This is not to say that we don't need pleasure, but it can be short-lived and, it is argued, mindless. In other words, 'flow' requires more mental energy and effort but is, ultimately, more rewarding and leads to increased skill and challenge because the activities are more complex.

Csikszentmihalyi claims that flow means that all the brain's available inputs are occupied with one activity. This means, of course, that it is impossible for negative and chaotic thoughts to come charging into your head.

He says that the mind 'with nothing to do, begins to follow random patterns, usually stopping to consider something painful or disturbing. Unless a person knows how to give order to his or her thoughts, attention will be attracted to whatever is most problematic at the moment: it will focus on some real or imaginary pain, on recent grudges or long-term frustrations.'

So the mind with nothing to do becomes a mind full of negativity, whereas a mind in a state of flow is so engaged there is no room for undesirable thoughts. The more flow activities that you have in your life, the more rewarding and happy your life will be.

 Basically, I no longer work for anything but the sensation I have while working.

Albert Giacometti

Are you doing a job you enjoy?

The more hours of the day that you spend in 'flow' activities, the easier it is then to be a positive person. The ideal would be to find someway of making a living doing something that not only engrosses and absorbs you, but also gives you room to grow and progress. Does your present vocation meet these criteria? Can you think of an occupation that you would enjoy that would keep you captivated yet challenged? For me, it is teaching – but this may not be your idea of the perfect job. According to the annual Happiness Index compiled by the City & Guilds Qualifications Board the happiest workers are blue-collar workers. Of those the happiest are beauticians and hairdressers, who gave as their reason the fact that they had an interest in what they do for a living and said that they believed this was the most important factor for on-the-job happiness. Teachers were ranked sixth – equal with accountants and marketing and public relations. You can check your own occupation at www.cityandguilds.com.

Another survey of 3,000 adults, conducted by the national training provider, Lifetime, revealed 48 per cent of UK workers regularly feel unhappy in their jobs. Two-thirds of those questioned said that their job 'paid the bills' and provided little joy in their lives; 61 per cent said that, if they had a magic wand, they would wish for a new career. Twice as many office workers said they were unhappy compared with those who had more active jobs; two-thirds of those polled said that they believed they would only be truly content at work if they were self-employed (www.lifetimehf.co.uk).

Of course, it is difficult to find, or even train for, another job during times of economic recession. Job security is a high priority – 70 per cent of those who said they were unhappy added that they would hesitate to make a career change – and someone has to pay the bills. But if you are unhappy at work and spend eight hours a day, five days a week there, it is a large proportion of waking life to spend doing something that doesn't suit you.

If you do decide that your work makes you miserable and that you need to do something about it – don't resign – that's not positive thinking. You need a plan of escape to make sure that you don't fall into the trap of negative helplessness: 'There's nothing I can do; there are no jobs.'

Use the steps in this chapter to help you to draw up an action plan. It may be a long-term plan, involving saving money in order to retrain, but you will feel more positive by working towards a goal rather than just accepting that these are the cards that fate has dealt you.

Deciding to make the best of the job that you have can also be a positive decision. You have to focus on what you are good at and be determined to do something about the areas that are not satisfactory. Again you need a plan. Ask for help and advice. As soon as you face a challenge and decide to do something about the things that aren't going well, you will feel a sense of being in charge of your own destiny – instead of allowing other people to pull the strings.

Remember, being positive doesn't mean putting a smile on your face and letting people walk all over you; it means taking responsibility for your own life and leading it according to your values and beliefs. Don't be afraid of what other people think – people may not like it when you stand up for yourself – but that's their problem, not yours.

> remember, being positive means taking responsibility for your own life and leading it according to your values and beliefs.

What else can you do that you enjoy?

Whatever your job, to feel more positive it's a good idea to deliberately introduce to your life activities that stimulate and interest you – at least three hours a week – but probably more if you are unhappy at work. The word 'hobby' has become old-fashioned but most hobbies fit the bill. They are chosen from a genuine interest and have nothing to do with work or payment. Choose a range of activities that are both creative and challenging – this does not mean that you will be in a constant state of excitement – rather that you will be absorbed, calm and content.

brilliant example

When Jan's daughters left home she decided that she wanted to reduce her hours as a social worker and to spend more time fulfilling some personal ambitions and dreams. She had played the clarinet for two years when she was at secondary school and decided that she would like to take it up again. She had individual lessons and then saw a card in the local library about an amateur band that was being formed.

She joined the band and now – ten years later – plays in four different music ensembles, having also taken up the alto and tenor saxophones.

She says, 'I love playing in the bands and have made many new friends by learning to play – although that hadn't been my intention.'

For many years, Jan has been fascinated by textiles and has been making small pictures and cards at home. Last year, she enrolled with the Open College of the Arts (www.oca-uk.com) to study textiles as a correspondence course. She has a tutor and is given assignments which she posts off and then receives feedback and suggestions.

Jan plans to retire in a few years; she had plans to do a landscape gardening course, but has decided she may just enjoy using her own creative ideas to transform her large garden into a place of wonder and tranquillity.

Hobbies

The mental health charity MIND suggests that, from their research, the most effective activities for feeling positive are: listening to music, gardening, writing, painting and drawing, drama, writing and reading poetry, crafts, walking, needlework or knitting and dancing. Add to these playing sport, playing a musical instrument, singing and reading, and you should find enough to keep you in the 'flow' and banish negativity from your life.

You may already see the difference between the kind of activities that make you feel fulfilled and happy and those that simply bring pleasure. Delayed gratification is often needed for a feeling of positivity and long-term happiness. In other words, you have to put some effort into it – like studying for a degree, or gardening. Whereas pleasurable activities are usually immediately gratifying and tend to be ones where we are entertained (watching television) – rather than doing the entertaining (acting); where we are passive or have things done to us (being on a fairground ride) – rather than being active (playing a sport);

where we are the receivers of creativity (shopping) – rather than doing the creating ourselves (cooking). Some activities (like sex) can, of course, be either. Or both. The happiest people manage to combine both pleasure and 'flow' activities in their lives.

brilliant tip

Watching television, apart from exceptional programmes, tends to be just a pleasurable way of relaxing and distracting your brain from thinking or worrying. According to Csikszentmihalyi, people score a low level of happiness while watching television (whereas reading gets high marks). It can be quite hypnotic once you start watching and, if you now feel inspired to take up other activities, just get into the habit of recording everything you want to watch. It makes you think about what is worth your time and also means that you watch what you want to watch, when you want to.

Reading

Researchers at Oxford University have been researching the effects of hobbies on over 17,000 men and women who were born in 1970. They were asked, at the age of 16, which activities they did in their spare time for pleasure (they included sport, cooking, going to concerts, reading and socialising). Their answers were then checked against the jobs that they were doing 17 years later. They discovered that they were significantly more likely to be in a managerial or professional role if they had listed reading for pleasure (at 16), compared with those who had not mentioned it at all.

Reading can, of course, mean different things to different people. Reading magazines and light fiction can be pleasure, whereas more challenging fiction and non-fiction will engross you and make you think and thus fit the definition of 'flow'. If you have got out of the habit of reading because you 'haven't got the time', try some of the books recommended on the website www.goodreads.com and post some of your own suggestions.

> Research by the National Literacy Trust, in December 2010, showed that three in ten children live in households without a single book. They found that these children were two-and-a-half times more likely not to reach the expected reading level for their age. Their research indicated that these children had lower levels of attainment and negative attitudes to reading in any form – this included sending emails and engaging with social networking sites.
>
> In my experience of teaching English (and also running school libraries), reading fiction helps develop emotional intelligence as it allows children to live experiences in their imagination. Children who don't read often become adults who don't read – but it's never too late to develop the habit.

Most libraries have their catalogue available on their website, although browsing the shelves will lead to new discoveries. It doesn't matter if you don't like what you have chosen – take them back and get some more – it's free. If you already own lots of books that you'll never read again try the website www.GreenMetropolis.com which allows you to sell your books online for nothing (and 5p from every sale goes to the Woodland Trust). If you are not already a reader there's a whole world of pleasure out there in books just waiting for you.

Does shopping count?

It's fun to have pleasurable activities in your life, but it is not the same as feeling positive and happy. Shopping, for example, gives a lot of people pleasure. But, often, the pleasure is short-lived and comes at a price. A study of more than 3,000 women, conducted for the Clothes Show Live in 2010, revealed that women devote more than 598 hours a year to hunting for the latest clothes and accessories and spend more than £1,000 a year. The producer of the show, Maryam Hamizadeh, said, 'Over their lifetime, women spend the same amount of time shopping as they do at secondary school.'

In her book *To Die For: Is Fashion Wearing Out The World?* Lucy Siegle writes that the average woman buys half her body weight in clothes every year and has four times as many clothes in her wardrobe as she would have had in 1980. She says that most women have at least 22 garments in their wardrobes that they have never worn.

Another survey by the PromoCodes website (www.promocodes. co.uk) found that two-thirds of the women they surveyed regret spending the money as soon as they get home; nearly a quarter said that they panic and break into a sweat when they realise how much they have spent. Women justified their purchases by saying: 'It was in the sale' or 'I needed cheering up' or 'I deserved to treat myself.' Most of the women said that they made excuses to make themselves feel better as they knew that they couldn't really afford it.

This is because the rush of pleasure that people get from making the purchase (dopamine) lasts for only about 90 seconds and in order to get the same feeling again there has to be another purchase. And then another. The result? Arriving home with purchases that you never intended to make and which you know that you can't afford. This is why you see celebrities laden down with designer bags after mammoth shopping sprees: they enjoy the dopamine rush, but as soon as it disappears they have to keep on repeating the process. Often these garments are never worn; before they are even unpacked, the pleasure of buying them is over and forgotten.

It is what Marx called 'commodity fetishism'. In plainer language, it is buying things for the sake of it. It is fashionable to talk about 'decluttering' and to feel virtuous when you have had a clear out of unwanted items. Of course, the way to feel like this all the time is to not buy so much in the first place. Celebrities might be role models for how to spend money – but they are not usually role models for how to live your life.

The Kindness Offensive

Part of living a fulfilling and satisfying life is to feel that you are making a difference to the lives of other people. This is one way of dealing with the feeling of frustration at the injustices in the world that are mentioned in the next chapter. Instead of feeling helpless when things go wrong and disasters happen far-away you can feel more positive about yourself by regularly making a difference on a local scale.

The 'Kindness Offensive' is a project which was formed by three young men (Benny Crane, David Goodfellow, James Hunter) in 2008, with the aim of 'having fun doing good'. They began by asking people what they could do for them and then begged favours from large companies. The project has spread (you can see some of their activities and talks on YouTube – such as 'NSPCC Kindness Offensive' and 'Kindness Offensive Toy Run') and in December 2010 they performed the world's largest ever 'Random Act of Kindness' by giving away food to 50,000 people, a toy for every child in hospital over Christmas, and warm clothes and sleeping bags to the homeless.

Volunteer

Other people have realised the way to make a difference is to volunteer to give your services to an organisation with which you feel an affinity. If you feel strongly about educational standards, become a school governor or volunteer at your local school. Raising money or volunteering for a charity that is close to your heart helps you to feel positive and be a useful member of society. Barnardo's, the children's charity, has seen a 12 per cent increase in volunteers in a year (17 per cent among those under 25). A visit to your local volunteer centre would show you the kind of work available and they would help you to match your skills and talents to the needs of the charities in your area (or try www.volunteering.org.uk).

Even the rich and famous can realise that there is more to life than just making money: Victoria Beckham takes her eldest son with her to do charity work in Kentucky, telling *Hello* magazine (20 November 2009), 'Brooklyn ... appreciates he has a blessed life and wants to understand and help those who have less than himself.' Trevor Sorbie has created a charity, 'My New Hair', which helps to design wigs for people who have lost their hair through cancer. Henning Mankell, Swedish author of the 'Wallander' books, works for six months of the year in Africa, where he does a lot of charity work including a project called Memory Books – which helps parents dying from Aids to record something of their lives to pass on to their children.

The charity Plan, which works with disadvantaged families and children in various poor areas of the world, asked seven established authors (including Kathy Lette, Joanne Harris and Deborah Moggach) to visit the places where Plan was working. The authors lived with the families and then wrote about their experiences, in whatever way they wished, and the stories were compiled into a book. All proceeds from the book, *Because I am a Girl*, go to the charity to fund further work.

Saving lives

In his book *The Life You Can Save*, the philosopher Peter Singer argues that to live in a country with plenty of food while others starve is morally wrong; that if we can prevent people from suffering without sacrificing anything of significance then why not do it. He poses the question of whether we would jump into a shallow, muddy pond to save a child's life. In the process, we know we would ruin our clothes and our shoes. We would all disregard this to save the child's life; in other words, we would prevent a child's death at a financial cost to ourselves. And yet, according to UNICEF, more than 10 million children die before their fifth birthday every year.

Giving money

In fact, of course, many of us already do give money: whenever there is a crisis or Red Nose Day, our consciousness is raised and we contribute with cash or our services. The Charities Aid Foundation estimates that the British public donated £10.6 billion to charity in 2010, giving more aid than ever to overseas disasters and breaking the record set in 2005 for the Indian Ocean tsunami. In the first 11 months of the year Save the Children spent £96.5 million on emergencies. The umbrella organisation, the Disasters Emergency Committee, allocated £106 million to the victims of the earthquake in Haiti and £64 million after the floods in Pakistan.

The *Sunday Times* Giving List for 2010 showed the 100 most generous philanthropists in Britain gave away £2.5 billion. There is a growing movement of philanthropy among the rich – people like Sigrid Rausing (heir to the Tetra Pak millions) who gives away £20 million a year to human rights causes. Whereas only 20 years ago 75 per cent of this country's wealthiest people had inherited their wealth, now 75 per cent of the richest are entrepreneurs who have generated their own wealth. It seems as if many of them, particularly those from modest backgrounds, wish to pay back some of their good fortune.

Toby Ord, an academic at Oxford University, pledged a third of his income to charity in 2009 and has guaranteed to give away ten per cent every year for the rest of his life. He and his partner, Bernadette Young, have set up a charity, Giving What We Can, encouraging others to do the same and have so far raised £13 million in pledges. Toby has calculated that with this money 29,000 premature deaths will be prevented (*Daily Mail*, 6 December 2010).

Brian Burnie left school at 15 to start work as a grocery delivery boy and ended up with a series of successful businesses. What makes Brian's rags-to-riches story different is that he has spent most of his working life raising and giving money to charities. Along with his wife and three children, he has hosted a lunch for 5,000 war veterans, barbecues for Tyneside Leukaemia, tea parties for Help the Aged, and lunches for Cancer Research. 'I've always loved making money. But I'd never spend it; I like giving it away too much. But it's easy writing cheques – you've got to get off your jacket and do something.'

In 2010, at the age of 66, he sold the family home, Doxford Hall – for £16 million – and auctioned most of the family's belongings, using the proceeds to start a charity, Daft as a Brush, which will provide a free bus service to take cancer sufferers to hospital. 'As my mother said: "You can only sleep in one bed at a time and only drive one car, and other people are in terrible need"' (*Daily Mail*, 6 November 2010).

Hello babies. Welcome to Earth. It's hot in the summer and cold in the winter. It's round and wet and crowded. At the outside, babies, you've got about a hundred years here. There's only one rule that I know of, babies – God damn it, you've got to be kind.

Kurt Vonnegut, *God Bless You, Mr Rosewater*

Small acts of kindness

The natural response when you hear that people have suffered misfortune is to want to give, or to want to help – or, in other words, to be kind. During the heavy snow in the winter of 2010, people reacted as they always do in an emergency and helped each other out. There were stories in the newspapers of complete strangers clearing snow to help a bride receive her wedding dress; of a farmer who used his tractor to drive midwives to and from hospital; of a Methodist church hall in South Yorkshire that put up drivers who had been stuck all night in their cars.

According to a study of 34 countries by the Organisation for Economic Co-operation and Development (OECD, 2011), Britain is near the top of a 'kindness' league table (but behind America, Ireland, Australia and New Zealand). People were asked about their 'pro-social behaviour': if they had given money to a charity or helped a stranger or volunteered in the previous month. The report 'Society at a Glance' suggests that Britons are more willing to help others, more generous and kinder than most other developed countries in the world (www.oecd.org).

The media directs our attention towards contributing money to humanitarian aid. But we can also use this altruism in our everyday lives. It is, of course, wonderful if you can spare the time or the money to give to good causes. But you don't have to wait for a disaster or extreme weather conditions to exercise kindness. Being kind on a more personal level can have just as much impact on individual lives. If you aim to do small acts of kindness every day, it doesn't stop you still giving when disasters happen. But it will make you feel as if you are doing something good with your life in a more enduring way.

When you feel positive about yourself, then you are much more likely to be kind and generous towards other people. Being kind to other people in small ways is always appreciated and rarely forgotten: a small gift when someone has had bad news; doing a favour for someone at work; offering to help out with a friend's decorating; mowing your elderly neighbour's lawn; or doing the chores for your flatmate when it's not your turn.

Positive people are aware of other people's needs and feelings. Remember: it costs you nothing to give a compliment, but if it is genuine it can make someone's day. Similarly, it shows generosity to praise someone's work or to thank them for work well done. And doing so improves relationships and creates good humour. We often have impulses to do good deeds, but fail to carry them out. Next time a kind thought crosses your mind, why not do something about it? What harm can it do?

In this way, a prevailing mood of selfishness, or meanness, at home or at work, can be changed into a general feeling of helpfulness and generosity. Acts of kindness spread outwards and permeate the atmosphere and it takes only one person to begin the process. Being considerate and kind to others in your daily life is one way to alleviate that hopeless feeling that you sometimes get when you hear the news. Making kindness routine rather than an occasional gesture is the way to make you feel more positive about yourself and your relationship with the rest of the world.

Action for Happiness

This is a new movement for social change pioneered by Richard Layard, Geoff Mulgan and Anthony Seldon. They believe that if we want to be happier then we must prioritise the things that really matter in life – including the happiness of other people. Those who join the organisation (which has no religious, commercial or political affiliations) pledge to produce more happiness and less misery. Take a look at their website www. actionforhappiness.org, which identifies 50 practical actions that people can take in their lives which would contribute to building better relationships and communities.

What's stopping you?

If you've just read this chapter and perhaps made a list of things that you would like to do, don't stop there. It is often fear of failure that stops people embarking on an unknown path. It may be that you feel that other people could do what you want to do in a better way. So what? It may be that you think you wouldn't be able to do it very well – you never know until you try. You may think that the reward at the end isn't worth the effort. Remember, however, that you are doing this for yourself and that you will enjoy the process if it is something that you really want to do.

brilliant recap

- Having aims gives you purpose and direction in life
- Working towards a goal is more important than attaining it
- A goal helps you to achieve focus and develop a positive attitude
- You have to define what you value and enjoy
- Purpose doesn't mean being selfish – your goals can be to help others
- Your ambitions need to be flexible and may change over time

- Purpose means finding activities that you take pleasure in and that absorb you
- Purpose means planning for the future and a positive life
- Small acts of kindness can make all the difference – it is your way of making the world a better place

CHAPTER 6

Stress, worry, anxiety:

How to confront your
demons

*The optimist sees the rose and not
its thorns; the pessimist stares at
the thorns, oblivious of the rose.*

Khalil Gibran

t's not just seeing the roses – or even smelling them – that shows the difference between an optimist and a pessimist. If you are in the company of someone who is negative or even just feeling a bit down, you soon realise that they can't focus on anything else. When you are stressed and anxious, it somehow consumes your whole being so that you don't notice, or enjoy, the beauty of the world around you.

In Chapter 2, we discussed how changing the language that you use affects the way that you think. In other words, action can precede thoughts as well as the other way around. So if you stand up straight, put your shoulders back, walk purposefully, with a smile (or at least a pleasant expression) on your face, you will feel better about yourself. Conversely, it is possible to make yourself feel depressed by walking slowly and looking down, shoulders hunched, with a miserable expression on your face.

Start noticing the way that people you admire stand and walk. People with a positive attitude have confident body language, without really thinking about it. To begin with, you may have to concentrate and constantly check yourself to make sure that you look positive about life. Try to be aware of how it makes you feel. Don't slouch or shuffle – walk purposefully – and look as if you know where you are going – and that you want to get there.

Laughing

When you are feeling worried and anxious, you have to look after yourself and behave in a counter-intuitive way. If peeling onions makes you cry, you may have noticed how the very act of crying also makes you feel sad. Similarly, if something makes you laugh, it leaves you feeling happy and positive afterwards. 'The Laughing Policeman' used to be a popular amusement arcade attraction in my childhood – it can now be seen on YouTube (although strangely it doesn't make me laugh now) but there are others that do. Try 'The Laughing Babies'.

Hearing laughter stimulates the brain region associated with facial movements. A great example of this is when, during the Second World War, they projected Charlie Chaplin films onto the ceiling of makeshift hospitals for the patients and discovered that even shell-shocked soldiers began to laugh.

If you're feeling miserable and the temptation is to stay indoors and wear your dressing-gown all day, it would be better to have a shower, get dressed in your favourite clothes, go outside, smile and speak to people – it will automatically lift your mood.

brilliant tip

Do you have a memory that always makes you laugh when you recall it? Try to remember the last time that you really laughed and recapture that feeling. When you next find yourself shaking or weeping with laughter, take note of the moment so that you can recall it whenever you need cheering up.

Listen to the birds

How long is it since you really listened to birds singing? Recent research by naturalists indicates that listening to birdsong elevates your mood. Peter Brash, an ecologist with the National Trust, says that listening to five minutes of birdsong everyday could be as beneficial to our wellbeing as a 30-minute walk or eating our five fruit or vegetables a day. The researchers played recordings of the dawn chorus to children at Alder Hey Hospital and discovered that it eased needle phobia and tension among the patients.

Are you already resisting this idea? (Notice how often you are resistant to any new idea; positive thinkers would give it a try.) Did you think, 'That's all very well, but I don't wake up in time to hear the dawn chorus; I'm trying to get my seven hours' or perhaps, 'I live in the city. I never hear any birds'? Well, let's think positively: if it's been suggested that just five minutes listening to birds each day can do you as much good as walking for half an hour, then it's worth trying. If you go to www.nationaltrust.co.uk and type in 'birdsong' you can not only listen to a five-minute recording of birdsong, but you can also learn from the site to distinguish the song of each of the birds (it could be a new hobby).

Why do people worry?

So let's imagine that you are eating well, getting at least 20 minutes of fresh air and exercise every day, you've tried listening to the birds singing in the morning, and you are working your way towards one of your goals. But still you feel anxious and worried. First of all, you need to assure yourself that you are not alone and that it is not unusual to feel like this. Some anxiety in life is inevitable and it can be good for you. A life with nothing to worry about would probably be boring. It is stress overload that damages your health and that you need to learn to deal with.

Surprisingly, it is not worrying about big things like terrorism and war that causes people to become overly anxious. In his book *The Confidence To Be Yourself*, Dr Brian Roet says, 'Small personal worries that leave some of us nearly paralysed with anxiety are replaced by this one big threat that puts everything else into perspective ... other worries won't have gone away, and as the immediate bigger threat recedes, a multitude of smaller worries fill the gap again.' It seems as if we have a certain capacity for worry and as one problem disappears it is replaced with something else.

So, if worrying is normal, why does it make some people ill? It is when your internal voice starts incessantly asking the question, 'What if?' and you find yourself going over and over possible consequences to the point that you become debilitated and almost incapacitated by anxiety. If this is the case, you may need to visit your doctor who could recommend counselling (or anti-depressants), but for most people just examining their worries in a calm and rational way may stop them reaching this point.

What do people worry about?

The energy supplier npower interviewed 3,000 people in Britain in December 2010 to discover what people worry about. The results showed that most people worry for a total of just under an hour a day. This adds up to two-and-a-half years of your adult life: two-and-a-half years wasted on worrying. 'Wasted' years because worrying is simply thinking about what might happen; it is feeling apprehensive about the future. Once the event has happened (or not happened), then we move onto something else and start worrying about that.

The top ten worries according to the survey were:

1　The cost of living.

2　Lack of money.

3　Illness.

4　Personal health.

5　Not being able to pay a bill.

6   Remembering to lock the house.

7   Having enough put by for a 'rainy day'.

8   Putting on weight.

9   Spending too much money on shopping.

10   Upsetting someone.

People also worried about skidding on ice and their boiler breaking down (the survey was during a cold snap). Many worried about other people: aged relatives, their children's happiness and performance, and their partner leaving them. Other worries included managing to keep the house clean, getting wrinkles, drinking too much, and being late for work. Money worries were the biggest concern: going into the red before payday and the cost of house prices were specifically mentioned.

How many from the list would be among your personal list of worries? Write down a list of ten things that are worrying you now. Put the date at the top. Do you think that it will be the same list in a month's time? Which worries do you think will still be on your list in a year's time? Were they on your list a year ago? Try separating your long-term worries from the ones that have occurred only recently. Group all money worries together and all health worries together.

Health and money worries

Long-term worries need dealing with, as they are not going to solve themselves. Sometimes, you just have to admit that you need help; the cost of an accountant or a solicitor

> sometimes, you just have to admit that you need help

might be worth it, if worrying is affecting your health. If your list does include health worries, then make sure that you have taken all practical steps to help yourself be healthy. Don't put off a visit to the doctor, hoping that things will improve. Ask yourself, What have I already done? Have things improved? What else can I do? Make sure that you are doing everything you can to improve your own health – re-read Chapter 4 for some ideas.

Solving money problems is usually a combination of spending less and earning more. What is certain is that the problems won't go away, if you just ignore them. Some people try to ignore bills and debts in the vain hope that 'something will turn up'. This is just wishful thinking – not positive thinking. Have you ever bought a lottery ticket (or bet on something) feeling convinced that this time you were going to be lucky? And were you?

The only way to solve money problems is to do something about them and, if you have a long-term problem, your first step may be to take advice from a debt counsellor. In the UK The National Debtline is free, confidential and independent (www. nationaldebtline.co.uk).

Take a cool look at the rest of your list and decide which worries are worth your time and which ones you cannot alter. You need 'to accept with serenity the things that cannot be changed, courage to change the things which should be changed and the wisdom to distinguish the one from the other' (Reinhold Niebuhr). For example, if your teenager has gone off travelling, and you have done everything you can to help, then worrying isn't going to make them any safer. Instead, concentrate on the things that you can do something about (such as transferring money to their account or planning a party for their return).

Worrying about the state of the world:

It is interesting that the top ten worries in the survey were all personal ones. Many people do worry about the state of the world but if you are in a good, positive state of mind you can listen to the news or read a national newspaper and respond appropriately to the reports of misfortunes and catastrophes at home and abroad. When things are going wrong in your personal life, however, and you are feeling negative about life in general, news of corruption, crime and disaster can just add to your feeling of hopelessness about the state of the country (or the world). You cannot turn away from what is happening elsewhere and surround yourself in a cocoon of pleasant events.

Being a member of the human race means being interconnected with everyone else and we are fortunate to live in an age when we are aware of what is going on in the rest of the world. Positive thinking may seem impossible when you hear news of natural disasters: floods, earthquakes, tsunamis – and man-made ones: another war, the effects of the recession, murder and mayhem.

We want someone to blame because we want to believe that we live in a just world where good things happen to good people and that those who commit crimes will be brought to justice and made to suffer. It is right to feel anger when you hear about murder, child abuse, the misery of poverty and fraud – not to do so would mean that you had lost something that makes us essentially human.

Positive thinking does not mean that you have the answer to the world's problems and feeling angry, worried or upset does not mean that you aren't a positive person.

Becoming a positive thinker then does not mean covering your ears and shutting your eyes on what is going on in the world around you. Neither does it mean being selective and only reading the 'good' news (although if you feel it is all you can cope with, at times, then you could visit www.guardian.co.uk/goodnews which only has good news).

It may mean, though, that if you want to protect yourself from the constant barrage of bad news then you have to examine the way that the news is presented and consider some strategies to prevent yourself from falling into the trap of negative thinking.

Think for a moment about how you are affected when you hear or read the news. It will rarely be good news and it would be unusual if it left you feeling uplifted and happy. What you have to learn to do is to analyse which items affect you the most and then decide whether it is worth your time worrying about them. If it is then find a positive way to take action.

Remember: when things stay the same or get better that isn't news. And that's good news. Bad news (but good for newspaper sales) is what is out of the ordinary, unusual or upsetting.

 **brilliant** example

The Spirit Level

In their book *The Spirit Level – Why Equality is Better for Everyone*, Richard Wilkinson and Kate Pickett produce exhaustive research from the wealthiest countries around the world. They measure the effect of income equality on the quality of life in the people in those countries.

Their data came from reputable scientific bodies such as the World Health Organisation and revealed that the greater the disparity there is between the top 20 per cent and the bottom 20 per cent of the population, the more social problems there are at all levels. In other words, the gap between the richest and poorest in society mirrored the levels of murder, obesity, drug use, mental illness, teenage pregnancy, bullying and anxiety.

They also found that the income gap was a sure indicator of the effectiveness and health of a society: Sweden and Japan were the least socially-divided, whereas the United Kingdom and the United States were the most (with a corresponding level of crime and ill health).

Don't waste your time worrying about things that are little more than scaremongering. Learn to spot the techniques the media use to manipulate you into thinking that a spate of similar incidents means there is a crisis. One example was the millennium bug, which was supposed to wipe out all our advanced electronic systems and cause chaos on the roads when traffic lights failed. Professor Ross Anderson, of Cambridge University Computer Laboratory, sent out hundreds of press releases suggesting that the problem had been exaggerated, but he says the media ignored these. When it didn't happen, no one sacked the doom-mongers. They just moved on to the next scare.

brilliant tip

If you do find that newspaper scare stories serve only to make you feel more anxious or add to your feelings of negativity, then make a list of any previous stories that you can remember. Health scare stories in the past, for example, have related to tea, lipstick, deodorant, plastic bottles, paint, broccoli, incense, phone masts and bacon. Add more as they occur (and they will) and then keep a note of whether the panic was justified. Look out for words like: 'potentially', 'could', 'possibly', or 'might.' They are not specific and tend to lead to exaggeration.

The many improvements to our daily lives in the last 40 years do not make news and are not the topic of discussion in the pub or at the dinner party. There are many things to worry about and lots more progress to be made, particularly for those at the bottom of society. But the actions of a minority – in terms of drinking, violent crime and drug use – are not evidence that society is falling apart. In fact The British Crime Survey (which can be accessed online and is published annually) shows that the overall crime rate is lower now than it has been since 1981.

The Culture of Fear

In his book *The Culture of Fear*, Barry Glassner suggests that we worry about the wrong things because the media misleads us. He believes that many situations are actually made worse by the fear the media creates. For example, he says that the whooping-cough vaccine scare in the 1990s was, in effect, a 'media-generated panic'. Programmes on television showed severely-disabled children and claimed that this was the result of the vaccine, claims which have since proved to be false.

Daily worries

If you find yourself still worrying over lots of minor problems, then make a resolution to write them down every night before you go to bed. Send yourself an email, if it is easier. There is something about writing things down that clears your mind and enables you to see the problem more clearly.

you have to accept that there are some things that you have no control over

Put a cross next to anything that you can't do anything about. For example, you can't do anything about the weather except to prepare and dress appropriately. Worrying isn't going to make the snow melt or the sun shine at the wedding. You have to accept that there are some things that you have no control over and that your worrying won't change. You prepare and do what you can – and then you sit back and do something enjoyable.

The things still remaining on your list must now be more immediate problems that you think you can do something about. For example, you may have had an argument at work that is causing an unpleasant atmosphere, or you may be unhappy at home because you feel that your partner, or children, aren't doing their fair share of the domestic chores. Again, nothing will happen, the situation will continue like this, unless you decide to do something about it.

Being more assertive could solve many resentments and atmospheres – in other words, saying what you think in a non-confrontational manner. If you are not used to being assertive, then it will take some practice and it is best to start where you feel most comfortable – perhaps discussing with a friend how frustrating you find it when she is always late. Remember the result, when you have been assertive, may not be that the other person will have changed – but that you will feel better for having expressed your point of view instead of smouldering and seething in silence.

 **definition**

'Stress'

Worry, then, is thinking about unpleasant things that might happen. Stress, however, is a mental tension that causes a physical reaction in your body. When you are stressed adrenaline is released into the bloodstream to speed up your reactions. Blood is then sent from the skin to your muscles to give them extra power and enable them to move quickly. This is the 'flight or fight' reaction, which was useful to your ancestors, but leaves you feeling irritable and unable to sleep if there is no physical release.

The main cause of stress is the feeling that you are not in control of your life. If you feel stressed even for a short time, it will affect your immune system and you may find yourself getting repeated colds, stomach problems, headaches, and muscle pains. Everyone feels stress at various times in their lives; it can be exhilarating and useful in dangerous or tense situations. Some people find they work better under stressful situations and that it makes them more creative and productive.

Too much stress for too long, however, is harmful to your body. Chronic stress is when you have been suffering for months or even years and your body is working overtime to cope. Quite often, people do not realise that they are suffering as they have become used to the feeling and it is not until they become ill that they begin to re-evaluate their lives.

brilliant example

Katy is the public relations manager of a large publishing company. She has received rapid promotion since joining the firm straight from university and is known for being punctual and always meeting her deadlines. She shares a flat with a friend, but is in a long-term relationship with her university boyfriend. She has elderly parents who are beginning to demand more of her time. She is on a permanent diet and goes for a run every morning before work. She also tries to get to the gym most evenings and at the weekend.

Katy has recently begun to have trouble falling asleep and she often wakes up in the middle of the night worrying about work, or her relationship, or her parents. She feels wound up and restless and has developed a tendency to get angry with her flatmate and jealous with her boyfriend. She has started to make mistakes at work, but becomes emotional and anxious when asked if everything is all right. She speaks quickly and is constantly tapping her fingers and jiggling her legs when she sits down. She often has a stiff neck and has developed backache, which she can't understand, because she feels as though she is exercising and eating correctly.

Do you recognise Katy's symptoms? She is frantically trying to fit everything into her life. Her instant reaction to her problems is to blame her flatmate or her boyfriend. She is behaving in an irrational way that is caused by stress but leads to anger. She is a perfectionist and has the words 'must' and 'should' running through her mind all the time. Her exercise routine has ceased to be healthy and become an obsession. She is on a perpetual diet and probably eats too few calories to sustain her energetic lifestyle and to enable her to sleep well. Her body is in a constant state of high alert, because of her stressful levels of anxiety.

What can she do?

Katy will probably keep on for some time trying to do everything until something forces her to stop. She will probably be off sick with exhaustion or, if she is lucky, someone will persuade her to take a holiday. When people work at this level of stress, they often fall ill as soon as they take a break.

There is an irony in trying to look after your body by spending time exercising and dieting but failing to look after your mental health. Chronic stress is the result of trying to do everything and being unable to prioritise and relax. To look after herself, Katie must first be prepared to admit her problems at work and then to ask for help from her family and friends. She has to learn how to relax and to include some fun in her life. Her exercise regime and strict diet also need to be moderated.

Learning to relax

In Chapter 5, we saw how just slumping in a chair and watching television does not necessarily stop your mind from worrying and thinking negative thoughts. It is not beneficial if you are still thinking about work or if you need to drink alcohol to block out troublesome thoughts and worries. Katy would probably say she had neither the time nor the inclination to take up an absorbing hobby, but she might be persuaded to spend some time with friends laughing and having a good time. This would have to be on a regular basis to have any lasting effect.

If Katy was a friend of yours, you would probably suggest that she uses some of the ideas in this book to help her to manage her anxieties and stress. You might suggest that she pampers herself with long hot baths, soft music, and scented candles. There are also other techniques for relaxing that might work for Katy – but she would have to cut back on her workload and commitments as well. There is no point going for a massage for the stiff neck and backache if she just goes back to work and carries on as before.

Meditation

One way that Katy could help herself would be to practise meditation. Meditating every day, even just for 15 minutes in the morning, has a calming and peaceful effect. Meditation techniques are divided into two types: one where you concentrate on something outside yourself like the flame of a candle or a mantra; the other has a broader 'non-concentrative' focus, like the sounds in your environment or your own breathing. The idea is to bypass the constant stream of chattering thoughts and to quieten your mind.

You can use a simple breathing meditation, like the one suggested in Chapter 4 to help calm the mind when trying to get to sleep. The only difference is that you are not trying to get to sleep, so it is better if you sit somewhere with your back straight. This can be the traditional cross-legged position or you can sit on a chair with a straight back, if you prefer. It must be quiet with no distractions.

Now close your eyes and concentrate on breathing through your nose. Breathe normally, but concentrate on the breath as it enters and leaves your nostrils. At first, it will seem as if your mind is totally crowded with thoughts. The trick is not to let your mind wander off and follow the thoughts, but to remain totally focused on breathing in and out. Practise this first of all when you are feeling calm and you will discover that it is possible to let your thoughts die away until you have nothing on your mind except your own breath.

With practice, you will discover a sense of inner calm and serenity that stays with you throughout the day. When you are relaxed and peaceful, stay in this state for a while as it allows your mind to rest and everything will feel clear and quiet. Afterwards, you will feel refreshed and by doing this on a daily basis you will feel better able to cope with life's problems and tensions. You may feel better disposed towards other people and your anger and irritations will diminish.

Mindfulness

 Do not dwell in the past, do not dream of the future, concentrate the mind on the present moment.

Buddha

Mindfulness, like other meditative practices, involves focusing on the here and now. Instead of worrying about the future and going over what has happened in the past, the idea is to appreciate the present. It is different from meditation, as there is no attempt to slip into an altered state of consciousness. Instead, it involves savouring what you are doing in the present moment. So, instead of eating your breakfast while checking your emails or thinking about work as you walk to the bus, you focus on what is going on at that very moment. Savour the taste of the breakfast; feel the freshness of the air; and listen to those birds!

Being mind*less* is the negative trait we observed at the beginning of the chapter: it is walking in the countryside so obsessed with your own worries and frustrations that you fail to appreciate anything around you; it is visiting a new city but spending all your time planning where you are going to go next; it is lying on the beach going over what you wish you had said. It is life passing you by without you realising it. As John Lennon famously sang, 'Life is what happens to you while you're busy making other plans.'

Practising mindfulness calms you down and makes you respond thoughtfully, rather than automatically, to what is going on. It makes you feel more connected to other people, so that you are more aware of your reactions to them. When you feel serene in this way, you are less likely to be aggressive and more likely to feel empathic towards others. When you start practising mindfulness, you will have increased self-control, as you won't be mindlessly eating a biscuit, or driving on autopilot, or re-reading the same page because your mind has wandered to some irritation earlier in the day.

Mindfulness is seeing the world with fresh eyes, no matter how many times you have travelled the route, or seen the view, or looked at a face. It is the habit of observing things anew and the more you notice, the more enjoyable it becomes. You can become mindful right now. Just tap into your senses and be aware of what is going on around you. It is not a goal that you need to achieve; it is simply a matter of paying attention to what you are experiencing at the moment.

You can begin by pausing at various times in the day and registering how you are feeling and what you are experiencing. For example, right now are you comfortable? Warm? Engrossed? Be aware of and appreciate your mood. Do this frequently over the next few days: when you are in the cinema, shopping, waiting in a queue, or sitting opposite a friend in a coffee bar. Just pause and savour the moment. Get into the habit of noticing, with new eyes, what you have previously taken for granted. Too often we look back and say, 'I was happy then – but I didn't realise it at the time.' We look at photographs and smile wistfully at how we used to be. Make sure that you enjoy and appreciate your life now – not in retrospect.

> get into the habit of noticing, with new eyes, what you have previously taken for granted.

You have to accept whatever comes and the only
important thing is that you meet it with courage and
with the best that you have to give.

Eleanor Roosevelt

Acceptance

Another tendency that negative thinkers have is either to go
over and over unpleasant things that have happened, or to avoid
thinking about painful things, so that they fester in the mind and
never go away. If you are thinking negatively, then you believe
that you are uniquely unfortunate – that no one else has suffered
such unhappiness, or unfairness, or injustice. When someone
dies, or a relationship breaks up, or you are the victim of a crime,
or you lose your job, you can be overwhelmed by the feelings of
sadness or even anger. By fighting the feeling or trying to make
it go away – perhaps with pills or alcohol – you are prolonging
the feeling of wretchedness. It is as if, by going over what has
happened, you think you can somehow change the ending.

It is these thoughts that make you feel hopeless and as if there
is no future. When tragedies happen, you have to allow yourself
time to grieve before you can accept what has happened. It is
no good trying to be positive – something dreadful has happened and it would trivialise it to not admit this. There are five
recognised stages of grief that people go through when there is
personal loss: denial, anger, bargaining, depression, and then
acceptance. These stages can happen to you when any tragedy
occurs – from an unexpected death, to a physical attack, or some
bad health news. The stages don't necessarily all happen or last
for a certain length of time, but it can be useful to recognise and
understand what you are suffering.

In his memoir *Half a Life*, Darin Strauss tells of how, as an
18-year-old, he killed a 16-year-old schoolgirl who turned her

bike directly into the path of his car. Although he was cleared of any responsibility for the crash, he contemplated suicide and has 'survivor's guilt' about the death. In the book he says, 'Regret doesn't budge things; it seems crazy that the force of all that human want can't amend a moment, can't even stir a pebble.' (*Half a Life*, Darin Strauss, Beautiful Books, 2011.)

When something dreadful like this happens, it can change your view of the world: you no longer feel secure, you feel as if your world has tilted on its axis. It makes you re-examine your beliefs and values and, sometimes, who you are. All the sadness, pain and anger that you feel is normal: there is no way to escape change, disaster and disappointment in life. It is all part of being human. There is no prescription for grief; you have to nurture yourself and allow yourself time to grieve and deal with the disappointment of your loss – not only the actual loss, but also perhaps the loss of some of your dreams and plans for the future.

The solution is not to try to cling on or to ignore, but to tell yourself that what you are feeling is normal and natural. It doesn't mean that you like it – the feeling is there whether you like it or not. It means accepting that the situation is beyond your control: there is nothing you can do about it; there's no point in asking, 'Why me?' It has happened and no amount of worrying and stress is going to change anything. It means giving up your dreams of how you thought things were going to turn out and acknowledging that everything has changed. Only when you have fully accepted the reality of what has happened, can you see a future and begin to have new plans and dreams.

Acceptance can be a difficult state to achieve, but the practice of meditation and mindfulness will help. Accepting that what has happened is past enables you to live in the present and, consequently, to stop worrying about the future. You realise that what is going on in your mind are just thoughts – and you don't have to let them take over your life. Remember the good that you still have in your life. Count your blessings. Know that things have changed, but that life will go on. Acceptance means the realisation that nothing is ever going to be as it was before, or as you hoped. It is recognising that things are as they are right now.

brilliant recap

- Make sure that your body language is positive – it affects your thinking
- Have a store of funny memories that you can recall when you are feeling down
- Laugh more often
- Sort out your trivial worries from the real ones
- Be aware of your stress levels and do something about them
- Be prepared to try something different: meditation, mindfulness
- Learn to accept what you cannot change

CHAPTER 7

Anger and irritation:

Know (and control) your triggers

Anger is an acid that can do more harm to the vessel in which it is stored than to anything on which it is poured.

Mark Twain

According to a study in November 2010 conducted by 20th Century Fox to mark the new season of the comedy *Family Guy*, nearly 20 million people in Britain are not speaking to members of their family because of bitter family arguments. Most of these people said that they held their mothers responsible and eight out of ten said that it was female family members who had started the conflict. Fathers were named as the next most likely member to fall out with, followed by sisters.

One third of all the people polled called their families 'dysfunctional' and one in ten said they had refused to speak to someone in the family for more than 20 years. One fifth of the adults said that a family member had died before they had made their peace. Four in ten admitted that they were currently involved in a dispute with someone in the family. While most of these fall-outs were resolved within a year, one in five said that they had gone more than three years without talking to a family member.

What do you think it is that causes people to get so angry that they will not speak to members of their family for years, even at the risk of leaving things unresolved after a death? What can be so important that it is worth causing such misery and upset to the most important people in your life? What are the arguments usually about among your close and extended family?

What causes anger?

According to those polled, most of the family arguments were about money, favouritism, or disliking a relative's partner. Anger among family members is often the result of unacknowledged hurt feelings from childhood. The painful experiences of perceived injustice, rivalry between siblings, jealousy and loss when a child, can affect your attitude and behaviour as an adult. If not dealt with at the time, these feelings may lie submerged until something happens in the present which causes a reaction that seems out of all proportion.

Whether the anger you feel is a reaction to a family member, a friend, a work colleague, your boss or a stranger, the cause is broadly the same: *someone has hurt your feelings* by obstructing or harming your needs, belongings or self-esteem. Anger then is the result of your hurt feelings and your response may become a desire to get your own back on the person who has caused the hurt.

Anger is a universal human experience that we all feel, in varying levels of intensity, at different times in our lives. The mildest form of anger is irritation – often caused by the thoughtlessness of others (leaving the door open, forgetting to tell you about something, being late to meet you, rustling sweet papers in the cinema). But being irritated can turn to anger, if you think that the actions of the other person are deliberate. If your friend is habitually late, then you feel as if your needs and feelings are being disregarded and you will begin to harbour a sense of grievance, which could ruin the friendship if not addressed.

Anger is usually directed at a specific person, such as a partner, work colleague or neighbour. Even when the anger is caused by an external event, such as a cancelled flight or a traffic jam, people like to vent their fury on one specific person. So when we don't agree with government policy, we use one person to be the 'bogeyman'. The doctor in the hospital faces the anger of the relatives of the cancer patient; the police constable faces the fury of the robbed victim; and the shop assistant deals with the anger over shoddy goods.

For most of us anger is a short-term feeling triggered by a significant event. But if you find that you are angry most of the time, especially over things that in retrospect were minor annoyances, it could be worth exploring the root cause. Keep a close eye on this and use the people around you as a good way to gauge the level of your reaction. If they don't seem to notice or care about the situation, then it may be time to ask yourself what is really going on and to examine the effect anger is having on your behaviour.

> examine the effect anger is having on your behaviour

How do you express your anger?

When you are angry you may experience a racing heart, a feeling of heat, and a surge of adrenaline. It is how you deal with these feelings that matter. You are probably already aware of your own tendency to get angry – whether you get angry more often than most and whether the intensity of your feelings seem to outweigh the situation. Perhaps you consider yourself a person who rarely gets angry or someone who is able to deal with their anger effectively.

Not all anger is expressed in the same way. For some people, anger is explosive: they fly into a rage and shout, scream, swear and perhaps throw things and become violent. Others show repressed and often passive anger. An inability to express your anger in a measured, assertive way may lead to you being sulky, sarcastic, or even physically ill. Remember that one cause of depression is anger that is turned in on yourself, because it is repressed. Finally, there is constructive anger, which means expressing your anger in an assertive and beneficial way.

It is important to recognise the different ways that anger is expressed in order to understand whether you are dealing with your own anger effectively. As you read the following descriptions, identify any of your own behaviour and also any reactions to anger by people that you know.

brilliant definition

'Aggressive anger'

An angry person can lose all sense of self, sense of discretion and caution, so that they become aggressive and want to verbally or physically hurt the other person. When anger becomes uncontrollable and can't find an appropriate outlet, then it turns to rage, which is destructive, and can be catastrophic.

This manifests itself in bullying: shouting, threatening, pushing, and using power over the other person. It can also be deliberately hurtful: using foul language or offensive jokes, discriminating against others, using threatening behaviour, using physical violence and ignoring the other person's feelings. Sometimes, aggressive anger expresses itself as showing off: wanting to be the centre of attention, mistrusting other people, and being unable to delegate. People with a tendency towards aggressive anger are often selfish and insecure; they don't tend to help other people; they often accuse or blame other people for their own mistakes; and they will, for example, ignore queues and traffic etiquette. They can be fuelled with a sense of righteous indignation at some perceived injustice.

Another sign of anger is frantic activity: speaking, walking and driving too fast; spending money irresponsibly; working excessive hours and expecting others to do so as well. When levels of stress are too high, it often turns to anger and can be observed when people take their frustration out on some blameless object: they throw their mobile at the wall; thump the car; or smash a plate. Be aware of times when you find yourself swearing at other drivers while in your car; or when you find yourself in a queue with fury building up inside you because someone is taking a long time packing or chatting to the assistant. Take a deep breath and smile – it doesn't matter. And muttering to yourself, or anyone who will listen, will just increase your anger so that you won't be able to let it go when you get home.

Aggressive people can be unpredictable; they tend to punish unjustly; they may explode over something minor; they refuse to forgive or forget, but will remember past hurts. There can be a sense of enjoyment in this kind of rage, even without consciously realising it, and so the feeling is fuelled and perpetuated. Such anger is destructive and can lead to breaking things, hurting animals, substance and alcohol abuse, and the breakdown of relationships.

If you don't recognise any of these behaviours in yourself, it may be that you are in the habit of stifling your anger. Read the following descriptions of the way people behave who feel angry but who try to suppress it.

'Passive anger'

Many people are frightened by the feelings of anger and try to suppress and ignore them: the anger will still be there, bubbling away underneath the veneer, but to the outsider it will look like passive indifference. Some people seem to suffer from an almost permanent state of anger, which they hide, and so often seem to be tense, irritable or frustrated. Unfortunately, unexpressed anger has a way of revealing itself – sometimes by constantly criticising other people or by being habitually sarcastic and having a pervasively cynical view of life.

Alternatively, people who repress their anger sometimes have a critical view of themselves: they invite criticism and frequently

▶

apologise. They can sometimes be too helpful while refusing help themselves and can often be accident-prone. They may set themselves up for failure by choosing people who can't be trusted as friends and partners. They can become depressed, because their anger has no outlet except themselves. Repressed anger can result in a constant state of anxiety about trivial things, but a tendency to ignore serious issues. It usually means avoiding crisis and conflict by not arguing back, but still quietly fuming.

The apparent indifference of a person who feels anger but doesn't know how to (or is afraid to) express it means that they often leave other people to sort out the problem while pretending to be unconcerned. They stay on the sidelines, but may provoke other people to be aggressive by gossiping, talking behind people's backs, muttering, and even complaining anonymously.

The way a passive–aggressive person may deal with anger towards a partner is to stop speaking to them; pretend they are ill; flirt with other people; avoid sex; withhold money; be ridiculously house-proud; use alcohol or drugs excessively; sleep a lot or overeat. The end result can be similar to someone who gets aggressively angry: a great deal of unhappiness is caused and relationships are ruined.

Physical effects

The physical effects of anger can be just as harmful as the emotional ones. Anger can raise your blood pressure and affect your heart and circulation (leading to blocked arteries). Suppressed anger can affect the digestive system and may lead to heartburn, ulcers, colitis, or irritable bowel syndrome. It may also affect your immune system so that you catch colds and flu more often and your recovery from illness is slow. Joints and muscles can also be affected by inflammations and you may find that your pain threshold is lowered.

The survey results at the beginning of this chapter indicated that 20 million people in this country say they are not speaking to a close member of their family because of unresolved anger. But anger does not stop with the family. It often shows itself in the workplace with similar disastrous results. Look at the following example and decide whether the anger being expressed is passive or aggressive.

brilliant disaster

Chris owns and manages a hairdressing salon. He began as a trainee hairdresser at 16 and he has worked hard to achieve this position. He has six other stylists who work for him, but he has a rapid turnover of staff. This annoys him as he feels that as soon as he has taught them the ropes they leave and work for someone else. He admits that he is a perfectionist and that he can be a hard taskmaster.

One of his longest-serving members of staff, Terry, has just returned to work after a few days' absence and asks for a day off the following week to attend a funeral. Chris is angry that Terry's absence has left him short-staffed. He says that Terry can have the day off for the funeral, but without pay. When Terry forgets to replace some equipment, Chris swears at him in front of the customers. When another member of staff tries to defend Terry and says it was his fault, Chris begins to rant and says, 'You're all just as bad. None of you know what hard work is. You're lazy and unreliable – the lot of you.'

Chris is ambitious and he has worked hard to achieve his dream. At school he was bullied and this now makes it hard for him to trust other people and to be forgiving. Although he can be charming with his clients, he is often bad-tempered and irritable towards his staff and this upsets the atmosphere in the salon. He works long hours and expects his staff to do the same. He finds it difficult to apologise after an outburst, but tries to compensate by treating them all to an expensive meal.

Why do people over-react?

Chris probably suffers from low self-esteem because of the bullying that he suffered at school – and so Terry's behaviour causes him to experience similar feelings of being let down and hurt. People over-react because they don't know how to express tense, angry feelings in an appropriate way. They are unable to sort out the trivial from the things that matter, and so everything just piles up until they explode inappropriately. People who are stressed quickly become angry and are often irrational and over-dramatic in their response to things going wrong.

> people over-react because they don't know how to express tense, angry feelings in an appropriate way.

As you read the following situations, think about whether they would make you feel angry. Try to estimate the degree of anger that you might feel and give each one a number from 0 to 5 (0 = wouldn't bother you at all; 1 = irritated; 2 = annoyed; 3 = depressed; 4 = angry; 5 = furious).

What makes you angry?

1   Being excluded from an invitation to a social occasion (that you would have liked to have attended). ____

2   Hearing that a friend has been talking (unfavourably) about you. ____

3   Being passed over for promotion (for someone you think didn't deserve it). ____

4   Coming home to a messy house (caused by others – who are already home). ____

5   Coming home last – but no one else has started to
    make the meal.   ____

6   Being burgled.   ____

7   Your country invading another country.   ____

8   Missing the bus or train by a few minutes.   ____

9   Having your car scratched.   ____

10 Misplacing your car keys/mobile phone/glasses.   ____

11 Having your purse/wallet stolen.   ____

12 Being stuck in traffic.   ____

13 Being 'cut up' by another driver.   ____

14 Being short-changed.   ____

15 Cold-callers when you are trying to do something.   ____

16 Charity collectors in the street.   ____

17 Being criticised by your parents/partner.   ____

18 Being criticised by your boss.   ____

19 A friend habitually turning up late to meet you.   ____

20 Someone getting a parking space when you had
    been waiting.   ____

21 A domestic appliance breaking down.   ____

22 More than one appliance breaking down at the
    same time.   ____

23 Workmen not turning up when they said they would.   ____

24 Bad workmanship.   ____

25 Getting ill.   ____

26   Family member getting ill and you having to take
     care of them.   ____

27   Someone lying to you.   ____

28   Government cuts.   ____

29   Bad weather on your annual holiday.   ____

30   Your parents showing favouritism to a sibling.   ____

Are there any other situations you can think of that have made you angry in the last few months? How often do you estimate that you get angry in a week? In a day? How do you show your anger? Are other people aware of it or do you 'bottle it up'? Do you ever get depressed rather than angry? Hand over the list to someone who knows you well and ask them to say how they think you would react if faced with these situations.

Can you see a pattern or identify the triggers that make you angry? For some people it is unfairness and for others it may be criticism or loss of self-esteem.

How do you express your anger?

It may have been difficult for you to imagine exactly how angry you would get – unless any of these have happened to you recently. If you are feeling calm and serene right now, perhaps nothing on the list seems too annoying. It may be that some of these situations really would make you feel angry, but you are in the habit of suppressing your anger and so it is difficult to imagine how you would feel.

Look at the ones where you scored 4 or 5 – what do you do with that anger? How would you express it? Does it make you feel better when you have given vent to your anger? Does it hurt other people when you are angry? Can you identify times when your expression of anger has been inappropriate?

> Anybody can become angry – that is easy, but to be
> angry with the right person and to the right degree
> and at the right time and for the right purpose, and in
> the right way – that is not within everybody's power
> and is not easy.

Aristotle

So how can you express anger?

It's not feeling angry that leads to these problems and behaviours; it's what you do next. In itself, anger isn't bad – it isn't a negative force. It is a natural response when we feel cheated, violated, humiliated or hurt in any way.

In the past, anger was necessary for survival. It is an instinctive and natural reaction to want to fight back when you are hurt or annoyed – but it is not appropriate in every situation. It is possible to express your anger in a healthy and assertive way – so that you are not suppressing or denying your feelings, but neither are you lashing out and trying to get your own back. Remember: you have the right to request a change in someone's behaviour, if it irritates or upsets you. But you can do this with respect for the other person's feelings.

brilliant dos and don'ts

Assertive, positive people may feel anger, but they know how to express their anger and how to get their needs met. It is probable that the situations on the list that don't make you angry are the ones where you feel confident that you can deal with them calmly. For example, if you know how to deal with cold-callers effectively and politely, then this will not be a cause of anger for you.

▶

Don't

✗ Sweat the small stuff: The first thing an assertive person would do is assess the situation and decide whether it was worth the energy. Often, the reason for unwarranted explosions of anger is allowing things to build up. When you feel overwhelmed, learn to prioritise and only deal with what is important. Let the small things go. Look again at the previous list of situations and decide which ones you think are worth the fight.

Do

✔ Ignore incidents that you can't do anything about: That means most incidents while driving (being 'cut up', being stuck in traffic, and so on); otherwise, you'll arrive home every day in a state of rage. The weather, too, you can't fight. Parking spaces? Missed trains? Just shrug your shoulders; it's just not worth it. (Although a lot of stress could be reduced by setting off earlier; in fact, quite a few things on the list could have been avoided with forethought.)

Don't

✗ Do anything when you are tired or stressed: This is the time when you are most likely to over-react and to respond inappropriately. So counting to ten, walking away, and sleeping on it, is the way forward – if you know yourself and believe you need to calm down first. This doesn't mean you are not going to act – just don't send that email, or go marching into your boss's office straightaway. (This probably applies to the first five situations on the list.)

Do

✔ Look after yourself: If there are always rows when you get home from work, then insist you have some time to yourself. Make sure that you have some good times and that work and home life aren't constant battlegrounds. Deal with the problem after a good night's sleep, when you can talk calmly and rationally to your boss or family. Going for a brisk walk often helps to clear the mind.

Don't

✗ Jump to conclusions: When you are in a bad mood or feeling angry, it is very easy to allow yourself to think the worst. In the example, Chris is angry with Terry and therefore immediately blames him when he spots something out of place. In fact, people often make bad judgements and risky decisions when they are angry, because the anger causes them to lose their capacity to self-monitor and to observe things objectively. Take deep breaths and exhale slowly. Try counting backwards from 20 – anything to stop you saying something you will regret.

Do

✔ Slow down and listen: When you're angry, don't just say the first thing that comes into your head; it is possible to think calmly even when you are feeling agitated. Take your time, ask questions, and check that your tone of voice and body language aren't aggressive. Ask yourself if you are just getting angry for the sake of being right. Listen carefully to the other person and acknowledge their feelings (this would have saved Chris a lot of anguish). Put yourself in their shoes and imagine what impact you are having on them.

Don't

✗ Over-generalise or catastrophise: One reason that people work themselves up into a fury is because they take an isolated incident and convince themselves that 'everybody' is like that. Or something goes wrong and that's it – the world's against you. Chris sees one mistake as a sign that all his staff are 'lazy

▶

and unreliable'. Anger makes people think in a negative way, so they are less trusting and more suspicious. Beware of using words like 'never' and 'always', as they will make you feel as if there is no hope and that you are justified in being angry.

Do

✔ Admit you are wrong: You can dig yourself into a hole when you are angry. You can get carried away with the sense of power that is really bullying behaviour. And even when you can see you are wrong or that your anger is disproportionate, it is difficult to back down. Limit the damage by apologising and admitting you were wrong – even if you can't do it immediately. Later is better than never.

Don't

✘ Make 'should' statements: You may get angry because people don't behave in the way that you want them to. You have your own standards and expect other people to live up to them: the trains 'should' run on time; you 'should' have got that promotion; Terry 'should' be prepared to work as late as Chris. Angry people have less sympathy and tend to blame a person's nature and not allow any excuse for the circumstances (notice that Chris was not concerned about the funeral or its effect on Terry).

Do

✔ Remember the positives: Although it is difficult, it is possible to remember the good things that have happened during the day – even when you are upset. Chris could look around his thriving, busy salon and be proud, instead of always looking for faults. He could remember Terry's loyalty and all the times he has stayed late instead of focusing on his absence.

Don't

✗ Immediately fight back when you are criticised: Being criticised or insulted hurts our self-esteem and the natural reaction is to fight back with a denial or a counter-criticism. With practice, you can learn to think calmly about whether there is any validity in the criticism. Ask for examples or ask the critic to be specific. Be careful that your body language is not hostile.

Do

✔ Recognise your vulnerability to criticism and refuse to get into a verbal duel: Ignore insults – they are not worth your energy (all generalisations like 'lazy', 'mean' and 'hopeless' are untrue). If the criticism is valid and constructive, take it on board and thank the person giving it. Saying, 'You're right. I'll bear that in mind in future' or even 'Thanks for pointing that out' can be disarming – and certainly saves a lot of energy and misery. If, after considering the criticism (and perhaps asking further questions), you decide that it is not true, simply say, 'Actually, that's not true.' You don't have to give further explanation, and certainly not until you are calm and can talk about it rationally.

brilliant tip

If all else fails and you are still feeling angry, just write it all out or send yourself an email, detailing everything that has happened and how you feel about it. Just keep on until you run out of steam. Do not send it – or show it – to anyone else. You could save it – or you could just tear it up into tiny pieces, or delete it. It's over.

What about justifiable anger?

If, however, you have waited a few days, and you are rested and calm, and you know it has nothing to do with feeling self-righteous or revenge, and you still feel angry – then it may be justified anger and time to take action. For example, if you think there has been an injustice, or corruption, or a cover-up at work, then you are right to feel angry and to do something about it. Your actions must be planned and you will probably need the help of trusted colleagues to expose the wrongdoing.

> if you think there has been an injustice, then you are right to feel angry and to do something about it

Once you have gone through the list of situations that may make you angry and taken out the ones that you can't do anything about, then you are left with the important things that you do need to deal with. Being a victim of crime is a violation of your sense of self and it is right to feel angry. Just make sure that your anger isn't directed at the wrong person. Often, we are angry with ourselves for not taking enough care, but we live in a society where reasonable care should be enough and your anger is justified.

When appliances break down, it is annoying – but if you haven't looked after them or have had them some time, then it is inevitable that they will go wrong sometime. Things don't last forever and when a few things break down at the same time it's just bad luck – not fate having fun with you.

The repairers not turning up or not doing the job properly is a different matter. This means that you must decide what you want and then you must ask for it assertively. It is no good getting angry and delivering empty threats. You are much more likely to get satisfaction if you plan what you are going to say and are reasonable. If you use an organisation like Checkatrade (www.checkatrade.com), your recourse is to post your opinion on the website.

Being assertive with cold-callers and other strangers who accost you is easy: you just smile and say, 'No, thank you' and put the phone down, or walk on by, or close the door. You don't have to be aggressive and you don't have to give an explanation. Always do this, don't waste their time by listening: if you wanted a service, you would find it yourself – you don't need someone to ring you up and persuade you that you need something.

It's the situations with family, friends and work (1 to 5 on the list on pp. 134–5) that do need dealing with. Let's imagine that you've had a good night's sleep and you are clear about the issues and what has made you angry. Understand first of all that this isn't about winning; it is about expressing your opinion and channelling your anger in an appropriate way. Be realistic and decide what you would like the outcome to be.

Let's take the example of coming home last and no one has made a start on the meal (5):

- Choose a time and a place when everyone is calm and receptive (not when you have just got home from work).
- Say that there is something that has been upsetting you and that you want to be heard.
- Check that your body language is relaxed, but that you are not trying to ingratiate yourself by smiling too much.
- State clearly – but not aggressively – what has made you angry.
- Begin with, 'I feel angry because …' instead of 'You make me feel …'; it means you aren't attacking them, so they are more receptive to your complaint, instead of defending their actions.
- Listen to their response. Don't get into an argument and don't raise your voice.

- Say what you would like to happen in future: 'In future, I would like you to ...'

- Have an 'or else' in mind – but you don't have to say it. This is not a threat, but a promise to yourself that you will not let people walk all over you.

- Finally, thank them for listening – and remember to praise them when they do what you have asked.

You can use this process whenever you feel angry because your needs are being ignored. Use it when you are hurt by your friend's behaviour (numbers 1, 2, 19, and 27) and at work if you feel you have been treated unfairly (3).

(For more tips and guidance on how to be assertive try reading *How to be Assertive in Any Situation*, Sue Hadfield and Gill Hasson, Pearson, 2010).

Diffusing anger

Having examined how to express your anger in different situations, there will still be times when you feel angry but there is no way to deal with it in a logical and rational manner. For example, when someone gets 'your' car parking space or you discover, when you arrive home, that you have been short-changed. You may find yourself getting more and more angry and frustrated, and repeating the story to anyone who will listen.

This is a mistake. It used to be thought that it was best to give vent to your anger by throwing things or punching something. But more recent research has found that retelling or giving in to your anger actually makes you feel worse. If you do nothing your anger eventually dissipates – and it is only if you keep resurrecting it by going over and over what has happened then you continue to stoke the fire.

In his book *The Better Angels of Our Nature: Why Violence Has Declined*, Steve Pinker argues that we may be living in the most peaceful time in human history. He explodes the myths about mankind's inherent tendency towards violence and argues that all forms of aggression (including war, child abuse and gruesome punishments) have decreased and are widely condemned. The title is a quotation from Abraham Lincoln: 'the inner demons incline us towards violence and the better angels steer us away.'

If you find, after reading this chapter, that you are still constantly getting angry, then it may be time to learn some relaxation methods and practise the deep breathing described in the previous chapter. Yoga and meditation are recognised ways of calming down and, if you practise the techniques every day, you will be able to relax whenever you find yourself getting agitated. Some people find it useful to visualise a relaxing experience if they are somewhere that is too public to use these techniques. If nothing works and your anger is becoming more frequent, then it may be time to seek professional help. Consult your doctor, who may recommend an anger management course, or contact the British Association of Anger Management (www.angermanage.co.uk)

Remember, the idea is not to eliminate the feeling of anger; it is to learn how to change the way that you respond to it. Once you can get into the habit of expressing your anger in a constructive and assertive way, you will feel much more positive about life. You will also feel more in control of things that happen, physically healthy and your relationships will improve.

Being able to deal with anger assertively means that you will learn that on occasions it is best not to respond at all: when someone is being difficult, it is often just their mood and nothing to do with you – they want you to respond and by getting angry or upset you are giving them what they want. You are not suppressing your anger – just not wasting your time thinking about it.

brilliant recap

- You can't eliminate anger from your life. Keep a journal – it will clarify the problem
- Remember that it's okay to have different opinions to other people
- You can change the way that you express your anger
- Make decisions about whether the person or the situation is worth your anger – try not to take things personally
- Make sure that you are not just trying to get your own back and bearing a grudge
- Remember, anger is usually caused by hurt feelings. By reliving the situation you are perpetuating the hurt
- If your anger is justified, then do something about it – but have a plan of action
- If there is nothing you can do – accept it – and do something else. Go for a walk if possible

CHAPTER 8

Positive thinking, not magical thinking:

How to accept the ups and downs

Believe nothing, no matter where you read it, or who said it, no matter if I have said it, unless it agrees with your own reason and your own common sense.

Buddha

There is no mystical secret to positive thinking. It is a state of mind that anyone can acquire, if they decide they want to. It requires focus and a trusting, open mind that is receptive to opportunities and chance. It is nothing to do with superstition and magic, but is a rational view of how to get the best out of life. One of the defining characteristics of a positive person is the belief that nothing is impossible and that they can make the best of any situation.

One problem is that some people believe this without realising that to achieve your dreams and to cultivate a state of optimism and contentment can take hard work and perseverance. They'd prefer to think that there is a simpler way – that, like a fairytale princess, all you have to do is wish for something and believe that your wish will come true. They are like talent-show contestants who repeat the mantra, 'I really, really want this' – as if this is a substitute for years of practice and hard work.

> to achieve your dreams and to cultivate a state of optimism and contentment can take hard work

There are many organisations and individuals who capitalise on this way of thinking and try to sell people the idea that they have an easy way to happiness and personal fulfilment. Often these ideas are harmless and just give their followers a false sense of security and optimism. Sometimes, they are just a cynical attempt to make money from vulnerable people or those desperate for some direction and guidance in their lives. Read the following examples and decide for yourself.

Cosmic ordering

Cosmic ordering is the name coined by a German self-help author, Bärbel Mohr, who published the best-selling *Cosmic Ordering Service: A Guide to Realising Your Dreams* (2001) and formed The Foundation for Cosmic Ordering. It is based on the premise that a person can simply write down their wish list and wait for it to become reality. It is similar to an idea that took hold during the 1930s Depression and proposed by Napoleon Hill in his 1937 book *Think and Grow Rich*, which sold millions and is still widely available. These ideas were also adopted by American radio and television evangelists such as Reverend Ike in the 1970s, whose slogan was 'You can't lose with the stuff I use'.

The former disc jockey and TV show host Noel Edmonds credits 'cosmic ordering' for his return to television with his show *Deal or No Deal*. He had not had a high profile on TV since *Noel's House Party* in 1999; after reading the book, he wrote down a wish list of things that he wanted (including a wish for a new challenge) and then waited for the 'cosmos' to make it come true. On the show itself, contestants have to choose boxes with various sums of money inside and appear to believe that by the power of their thoughts they can choose the right box.

It is certainly true that those writing the books and making the television programmes have become rich.

Guardian angels

If you type 'angels' into Amazon, you will find that there are thousands of books advising you how to get in touch with your guardian angel. 'In the book world, angels have become the new misery memoirs,' says Jo Lal of Hay House publishers (interviewed in the *Sunday Times*, *Style* magazine, 29 November 2009). According to a 2009 Mori poll, 58 per cent of British women believe they have a guardian angel – with the majority saying that they have actually had help from them.

According to these books, these angels aren't the implacable angels we find in the Bible: they are there to assist with everything from finding your car keys, to losing weight, and finding the right man. Finding a car parking space seems to occur frequently. They are your very own guardian angels; apparently, others are also standing by, who can come in useful for the odd occasion when yours is busy.

Once again, the idea seems to be that you make an angelic shopping list to get all the things in life that you want. You have to be very specific in describing exactly what it is you wish for. Many of them suggest building an 'angel altar' – with flowers and crystals and incense or scented candles. Then you picture your angel and focus on what you want. Afterwards you look for signs, such as white feathers and rainbows.

It's big business for people who do 'angel readings', like Sabi Hilmi, who worked in the City and runs the Purely Angels website (www.purely-angels.com) from her 'angel sanctuary' in north London. Professor Chris French, a psychologist and angel sceptic, said on the Sky *Real Lives* Angels programme (21 December 2009), 'A while ago, it was alien abductions that fascinated people … There is evidence to show that people turn to superstitious thinking during hard times … The only real issue is that if you get too caught up in relying on angels for guidance, you are relying on something outside yourself to make it happen. It's far better to be the master of your own fate.'

The Power Balance Bracelet

A silicone bracelet – embedded with a 'healing hologram' and promising to 'rebalance the body's energy' – has sold 2.5

million: a must-have celebrity accessory that promised strength, balance and flexibility for £29.99. Worn by David Beckham, Kate Middleton and Robert de Niro, it has been argued as being no more use than a rubber band. Challenged by the Australian Competition and Consumer Committee, the manufacturers in the US admitted that it couldn't prove their claims and offered refunds to customers who felt they had been misled.

Statistician and broadcaster Michael Blastland, writing on the Sense About Science website (www.senseaboutscience.org.uk), says, 'People have their ups and downs. Sometimes the ups occur when they wear odd socks, sometimes a new bracelet. Give enough bracelets to enough people and some are bound to have a great day. That's just chance. And when you ask people to report the ups, it's the ups that tend to be reported. That's known as selection bias.'

Tarot cards, fortune-tellers, psychics

In 2005, Derren Brown, the illusionist, toured the US under a false name and convinced five leading figures in the field of spiritualism and fortune-telling that he had powers in their field of expertise. He said he was a practitioner in Christian evangelism, alien abduction, psychic powers, New Age theories, and contacting the dead. The idea was to show the power of 'confirmation bias' – that people hear only things that support what they already believe and that they ignore any evidence to the contrary. At each show, the entire audience was convinced of his abilities and failed to question his 'powers'. He had said that he would come clean if anyone accused him of being a fraud.

So convincing was Brown at 'hearing the voices' of dead relatives of people in the audience that, even when they were told later that it was all a hoax, many people refused to believe it and continued to have faith in Brown's ability to contact the dead.

In another television show, in 2006, Brown had 15 participants (from Spain, the UK, and the US) provide him with a small personal item. Brown instructed them to place these in a numbered envelope when he turned his back. He then left the group for an hour while he 'analysed' these items (as well as the personal object, they drew round their hands and gave him the time and date of their birth). He provided each of the participants with their personality profile and asked them to measure how accurate it was as a description of their character.

Out of the 15 subjects, three rated the description of their personality – in terms of accuracy – as between 40 to 50 out of 100. The rest gave a rating of 80 to 99. All of them were amazed and convinced that Brown had the power to gain deep insights into their character through his paranormal ability. Finally, Brown asked them randomly to exchange the envelopes containing their descriptions and then to read the one they ended up with and see if they could guess who it was. They were confused when they discovered that no matter how many times they shuffled the envelopes they always ended up with their own.

Gradually, it dawned on the participants (and the audience at home) that all the descriptions were exactly the same. They were incredulous: two of the participants just couldn't accept that they had been tricked and refused to discuss it; and another was convinced that the TV crew had read her diary. Brown discusses this trick in his book *Tricks of the Mind*.

It is based on an experiment carried out in 1948 by psychologist Bertram R. Forer and is often called the 'Forer Effect' or 'Barnum Statements' (after P. T. Barnum, an American showman). Forer's research indicated that people enjoy, or feel important, having their lives scrutinised or discussed. Particularly if the person giving the comments is someone in authority, or someone they respect, they will accept generalised comments and not consider whether they could equally well apply to almost anyone.

brilliant example

Below is the evaluation that Forer gave to his students (Derren Brown's was longer. It was compiled using descriptions of personality given for the different signs of the zodiac).

When you have read it, decide how convinced you would have been (by giving it a mark – out of a top score of 5) as an accurate description of your character.

> You have a great need for other people to like and admire you. You have a tendency to be critical of yourself. You have a great deal of unused capacity which you have not turned to your advantage. While you have some personality weaknesses, you are generally able to compensate for them. Disciplined and self-controlled outside, you tend to be worrisome and insecure inside. At times you have serious doubts as to whether you have made the right decision or done the right thing. You prefer a certain amount of change and variety and become dissatisfied when hemmed in by restrictions and limitations. You pride yourself as an independent thinker and do not accept others' statements without satisfactory proof. You have found it unwise to be too frank in revealing yourself to others. At times you are extroverted, affable, sociable, while at other times you are introverted, wary, reserved. Some of your aspirations tend to be pretty unrealistic. Security is one of your major goals in life.

In 1948, Forer's students gave an average evaluation of 4.26 and on the many occasions the experiment has been repeated since, the average has remained the same.

 **brilliant** definition

'Scepticism' not 'cynicism'

One of the reasons that so many people are taken in by 'cold' reading (when the predictions are made with no prior knowledge of the participant) may be that we like – and therefore accept – judgements made about our character if they are flattering. We also want to make sense out of the haphazard and random nature of events and are drawn to anything that seems to provide certainty and a sense of order in our lives. Once people believe, then anything that happens that apparently confirms the belief is seized upon as proof; anything that seems to be a contradiction is ignored.

Thinking positively does not mean that we have to have blind faith that our fate or destiny is preordained, and that there is nothing we can do about it. Quite the opposite in fact.

> thinking positively means being our own guardian angel.

Thinking positively means we have goals and the optimism to work hard towards achieving those goals and creating our own destiny, being our own guardian angel.

There is also no contradiction in having a positive attitude to life and also having a healthy scepticism about some things that your instinct inclines you to be wary of. A sceptical person will have initial doubts or curiosity about something and will then begin to question in a rigorous manner until satisfied that the idea is convincing – or not.

Being sceptical is different to being cynical, which suggests a tendency to be negative and to doubt the motives and sincerity of most people and ideas. A cynic's immediate response to an idea would be to find fault and to refuse to have an open mind – whereas a sceptic will have doubts, but retain a sense of enquiry and curiosity, which may be satisfied with proper evidence.

Sometimes, people are so desperate to improve their lives that they become victims of charlatans or trickery. In many cases this is harmless and such beliefs may provide some temporary comfort in difficult times. But, for some, it can be more dangerous.

Maitreya

You may have read about Dr Raj Patel, a London-born academic (with degrees from the London School of Economics, Oxford University, and Cornell University). He appeared on American television in January 2010 to discuss his new book, *The Value of Nothing*, which was about how to improve life for billions of poor people around the world after the economic collapse.

Unfortunately for Dr Patel, an 87-year-old Scottish mystic, Benjamin Crème, had, in the previous month, announced to his followers of the obscure sect Share International that their Messiah (called Maitreya) would shortly be appearing on American television. Crème said that a bright star would precede the appearance: immediately, there were reports on the internet from all over the world of just such a star.

Crème says that Maitreya represents a group of beings from Venus called the Space Brothers and has been resting in the Himalayas for 2,000 years. Since the footage of his television interview appeared on YouTube, Dr Patel has been hailed as the saviour Maitreya – despite his frequent categorical denials.

The similarities between Patel and Maitreya, as seen by the followers, are conclusive evidence: Patel travelled from India to the UK as a child (he was taken there on holiday at the age of seven); he grew up in London; he has a slight stammer; and he appears on television. The paradoxical proof, however, is the fact that he denies he is the Messiah – as it was prophesied he would.

In fact, Dr Patel rejects the idea of one person being a saviour. Interviewed in the *Guardian* (20 March 2010), he said, 'What I'm arguing is precisely the opposite of Maitreya … People are very ready to abdicate responsibility and have it shovelled onto someone else's shoulders.'

What about luck?

There can be no doubt that some people seem more fortunate than others. If you're a lucky person, you may have started life in a democratic country with clean air, a good health service, free education, reliable emergency services, and a legal system that enables you to feel safe and sleep soundly at night. If you're very lucky, you may spend your life in a country free from any major diseases, which is not at war with another country or suffering from internal strife. If you're incredibly lucky, you may have been born into a family which has provided you with love, a roof over your head and all the necessities of life. If you're a lucky person, you may also have made good friends, been on holiday, perhaps visited other countries, developed your own interests and enjoyed music, art, reading, the theatre, the cinema and sport.

When you find yourself complaining about your lot in life or comparing your own misfortune to the good luck that other people enjoy, remember that there are many people who would consider you to be a 'lucky' person. In his book *Don't Vote! It Just Encourages the Bastards*, P. J. O'Rourke tells the story of his 12-year-old daughter complaining to him that life isn't fair. He tells her, 'Honey, you're cute. That's not fair. You're smart. That's not fair. You were born in the United States of America. That's not fair. Darling, you had better get down on your knees and pray to God that things don't start getting fair for you.'

 **example**

Positive people are lucky people

Being lucky then is a matter of perception: it is said that people make their own luck, but it is also a different way of looking at life. People can suffer the most dreadful adversity and yet still consider themselves lucky.

Gill Hicks survived the London Underground bombing in 2005. She was the last survivor to be pulled from the wreckage and was so badly injured she was unidentifiable. Her legs were ripped to shreds; she lost 85 per cent of her blood and suffered three cardiac arrests. Speaking to Camilla Long in the *Sunday Times*, she said that she would not normally have been on that train at 8.50am as she was usually at her desk by 8am.

Instead of considering herself unlucky, she observes how she used her scarf as a tourniquet to stem the flow of blood as she waited for rescue: 'I very rarely wear scarves.' When asked why she didn't give in, when she realised that if she survived it would be as a double amputee, she said: 'The curiosity of being alive. What will I do? Life urged me to hang on. And that's why I've never had a moment of bitterness. I never think: why me?'

Gill Hicks thought she was lucky because she was wearing a scarf on the day of the bombing – which she was able to use as a tourniquet, thus saving her own life. She credits her recovery and attitude to life to the emergency services, 'who never gave up, risked their lives …' and her friends, who also gave her, 'unconditional love'. What is remarkable about people who think they are lucky is the ability to focus on the things that go right, to be grateful for what can be salvaged rather than dwelling on misfortune and bad timing.

Superstitions

So you may consider yourself born lucky or as just plain unlucky. But this has nothing to do with your star sign, or walking under ladders, or touching wood – these are just superstitions. There may be no harm in believing in these superstitions or the power of a bracelet or a guardian angel – if they have the desired effect of helping you to believe that you are lucky. It is when you rely on them rather than yourself that it can become troublesome.

The problem with relying on a superstition is that it can take away motivation and effort. For example, if you believe that everything is preordained, then you attribute everything that happens to fate. The logical effect of believing in fate is to sit back and let things happen – so if you go for a job interview you would just hope for the best, as you believe that the outcome is already 'written in the stars'. A positive thinker, however, would prepare well and practise: they would go into the interview feeling confident. This would affect their performance and so they would be more likely to be 'lucky' and get the job. If they didn't get the job, they would be able to see some positive outcomes (or would turn the 'bad luck' to their advantage) by making good contacts or perhaps realising that the job wasn't right for them.

 Luck is believing you're lucky.

Tennessee Williams

Things happen randomly. It happens by accident or chance that we are in a certain place at a certain time. But we can view everything that happens to us from a lucky person's standpoint – or we can decide that we are unlucky and the same events will be seen in a different light. So people who think positively usually regard themselves as lucky – but it is not a belief that everything will fall into their laps without any effort. It is a way of looking at events with optimism and extracting the best, whatever the outcome.

Nothing will stop life's ups and downs. There is no talisman to protect you from heartache and disappointment. But, with a positive attitude, you will know that these are all part of life. Learning from sorrow, mistakes and setbacks is the key to recovery and to realising that you have the strength and fortitude to go on.

feeling lucky and being a positive thinker are synonymous

Feeling lucky and being a positive thinker are synonymous, if we mean by being 'lucky' having an expectation of good fortune. They are also comparable in that you can train yourself to consider yourself lucky, by cultivating the habit of noticing and deliberately focusing on the upside of things that happen to you. Being lucky and being a positive thinker are the same if we mean that both lead to the feeling that the world is your oyster. It is possible to be happy in love and in work, and to lead a meaningful and fulfilling life. The choice is yours: think of yourself as lucky and you will be; visualise good things happening to you and they will; believe that everything will turn out well in the end and it will; and finally, adopt a positive attitude towards life and your life will be everything you want it to be.

brilliant recap

- There is no secret to positive thinking – it is nothing to do with superstition or magic

- People will believe anything in the hope that their dreams will come true – without any effort

- Have an enquiring mind: be sceptical and questioning – but not cynical

- Being lucky – like being positive – is a matter of perception: if you think you are lucky you will be

- Having a positive attitude towards life is your choice – and you can begin now

Conclusion

The robbed that smiles steals something from the thief.

Shakespeare, Othello

There is something in the human psyche that enjoys being miserable. We like listening to sad songs and watching sentimental films. It has been estimated that more than 40,000 books have been written about the end of the world. Every time the end of the world is predicted and it doesn't happen, it only confirms to the believers that it is their faith that has saved us. The 'disconfirmation' makes the faith greater.

There can be a tendency to drift towards a negative attitude and a series of disasters and upsets can cause a setback. If you have spent most of your adult life being a pessimist, you will not be able to change your attitude overnight. You may need to check yourself constantly to make sure that you are not lapsing into your old, grumpy ways. Putting the principles of positive thinking into practice takes vigilance and self-awareness until it becomes second nature. Remember: negative people give up too easily: don't allow the things that go wrong to confirm that you were right all along. Persistence is all part of being positive.

> persistence is all part of being positive.

While writing this book, we were burgled and my laptop computer (with nearly half of the book completed) was stolen. And no, it wasn't backed up. The house was ransacked and the last pieces of my mother's jewellery were stolen. I was angry and raged at the injustice of it all (I had stayed late at school helping students finish their GCSE coursework while the burglars were at work in the house).

By the next day I had calmed down, gone out and bought a new computer, and started all over again. That's life. No one can sail through life with nothing bad happening to them. It is how we deal with unexpected events that matter. There is no point ranting and raving and deciding that the world is against you. Some things you just have to accept and move on. If you are a positive thinker you can see something hopeful in even the darkest times. This book isn't the same one that I wrote before the burglary; it is different and the experience certainly made me more aware of my own levels of anger (most of the situations in Chapter 7 are ones that happened to me while I was writing it).

If you have become a habitual negative thinker, it's difficult to change – and it won't happen overnight – you'll have lots of slips along the way. But it is possible.

Like most things in life, there will never be an end result when you will say: 'That's it. I'm a positive thinker.' But there will be many times when you realise that you are happier than you used to be: you have learned that your way of thinking and seeing things is entirely up to you. You can choose to be miserable, negative and pessimistic about life and things that happen to you. Or you can welcome life with all its messiness, upsets and triumphs as something to celebrate – because that's what life is.

> you can welcome life with all its messiness, upsets and triumphs as something to celebrate

Decide now that this is your life and you are going to live it in the best way possible: by looking after yourself, being involved and kind to other people and having a positive frame of mind which welcomes everything life has to offer you.

Further reading and references

Here's a list of some of the books and websites mentioned which you might enjoy:

Athill, D. (2008) *Somewhere Towards the End*, Granta Books

Bronson, P. & Merryman, A. (2010) *NurtureShock*, Ebury Press

Brown, D. (2006) *Tricks of the Mind*, Channel 4 Books

Csikszentmihalyi, M. (1992) *Flow*, Rider

Eagleman, D. (2011) *Incognito: The Secret Lives of the Brain*, Canongate Books Ltd

Forer, B. R. (1949) 'The fallacy of personal validation: A classroom demonstration of gullibility' *Journal of Abnormal and Social Psychology*, 44, 118–123

Glassner, B. (2000) *The Culture of Fear*, Basic Books

Hadfield, S. & Hasson, G. (2010) *How to be Assertive in Any Situation*, Pearson Education

Hasson, G. & Hadfield, S. (2009) *Bounce: Use the Power of Resilience to Live the Life You Want*, Pearson Education

Middleton, C. & Drake, T. (2009) *You Can be as Young as You Think*, Prentice Hall Life

Pinker, S. (2011) *The Better Angels of Our Nature: Why Violence has Declined*, Viking Adult

O'Rourke, P. J. (2010) *Don't Vote! It Just Encourages the Bastards!*, Grove Press

Seligman, M. (2011) *Flourish*, Nicholas Brealey Publishing

Singer, P. (2010) *The Life You Can Save*, Picador

Strauss, D. (2011) *Half a Life*, Random House

Wolpert, L. (2011) *You're Looking Very Well: The Surprising Nature of Getting Old*, Faber & Faber

www.nationaltrust.co.uk (type in 'birdsong')

www.guardian.co.uk/goodnews

www.actionforhappiness.org (Richard Layard, Geoff Mulgan and Anthony Seldon)

www.authentichappiness.sas.upenn.edu (Martin Seligman)

www.howdidyousleep.org

www.angermanagement.co.uk

www.ons.gov.uk/well-being (Office for National Statistics 'Well-being' index)

www.cityandguilds.com (Happiness Index of occupations)

www.lifetimehf.co.uk (survey of job-related happiness)

www.oca-uk.com (Open College of Arts)

www.freecycle.org

www.GreenMetropolis.com (allows you to sell your books online for free)

www.goodreads.com

www.nationaldebtline.co.uk

www.checkatrade.com

www.senseaboutscience.org.uk (Michael Blastland)

www.economist.com/node/15452867 (article based on the annual British Crime Survey, showing that things aren't as bad as we think)

www.ted.com (Sarah Kay's 'If I should have a daughter ... 10 things I know to be true')

On YouTube: 'NSPCC Kindness Offensive', 'The Kids' Marshmallow Experiment', 'The Laughing Babies' and 'Liz Murray from Homeless Teenager to Harvard'

And finally: OhLife.com – the online diary which will enable you to keep track of your progress as a positive thinker. Good Luck.